HISTORIC TALES
= of =
OAK BLUFFS

SKIP FINLEY

Published by The History Press
Charleston, SC
www.historypress.com

Copyright © 2019 by Skip Finley
All rights reserved

On the Cover (*clockwise*): Herbert L. Jackson and Adam Clayton Powell Jr. *Courtesy of Lance Pope*; Uncle Nathan. *Courtesy of the Martha's Vineyard Museum*; Lucy Hart Abbot. *Courtesy of Martha Abbot, photograph by Sam Low*; Ocean Park Bandstand. *Courtesy of Vineyard Colors*.

Opposite: Ewell W. and Mildred J. Finley. *Author's Collection.*

First published 2019

Manufactured in the United States

ISBN 9781467143974

Library of Congress Control Number: 2019939725

Notice: The information in this book is true and complete to the best of our knowledge. It is offered without guarantee on the part of the author or The History Press. The author and The History Press disclaim all liability in connection with the use of this book.

All rights reserved. No part of this book may be reproduced or transmitted in any form whatsoever without prior written permission from the publisher except in the case of brief quotations embodied in critical articles and reviews.

This is dedicated to my parents, Ewell W. Finley (1924–1979) and Mildred V. Finley (1924–1984), who were able to acquire a summer home in Oak Bluffs on Martha's Vineyard Island for their family in 1955. Growing up in the fifties, few people and almost no black folks could make that claim—and I'm grateful. They were able to do so thanks to my dad having founded the nation's largest black-owned civil engineering firm, which participated in the design of many highly visible projects.[1]

My mom, an athlete (tennis, golf, yoga and judo), socialite and homemaker, met my dad at Howard University, where they attended college and he got his undergraduate degree before earning his master's in engineering at the University of Michigan.

They were two of many unique people of all races fortunate enough to discover the town of Oak Bluffs—and leave it to thankful children.

CONTENTS

Acknowledgements	11
Introduction	13

CHAPTER ONE

My Story	15
Ann Margetson (December 28, 1931–April 20, 2014)	15
Foundations	19
Discovery	20
Contact	20
New Religion	21
Governor Thomas Mayhew	21
Thomas Mayhew Jr. and Hiacoomes	22
Pulpit Rock	23
Geography and Geology	26
The Barbary Coast	27
Early Economics	28
Methodism	29
New Beginnings	29
Ichabod Norton and Old Harry	29
The Azores	30

Contents

Chapter Two
Abolitionists	31
Jeremiah Pease (April 8, 1792–June 5, 1857)	31
Reverend Hebron Vincent (1805–1890)	33
Robert Morris Copeland	34
Ebenezer Lamson (1814–1891)	35
Ichabod Norton Luce (1814–1894)	35
Edward Dobbs Linton	36
Frederick Douglass	37
William Claflin and Hiram Rhodes Revels	37
Gilbert Haven	38
City in the Woods: Prayers for All	39
The Captains of Cottage City: 1866–74	39
The Partners	41
William Bradley (1825–1895)	41
Captain Shubael Lyman Norton	41
Grafton Norton Collins (1820–1889)	42
Ira Darrow (1799–1871)	42
The Off-Islanders: E.P. Carpenter and William Hills	43
Triumph, Disaster and Secession	44
Katama and the Railroad	45

Chapter Three
The Panic of 1873	47
Cottage City	48
The End of the Oak Bluffs Land and Wharf Company	50
Charles Tallman	51
Bathing and Beaches	53
Real Estate and Neighborhood Developments	54
Lucy Vincent Smith	55
Iconic Architects and Architecture	58
Ellen Weiss	58
Robert Taylor	58
Samuel Freeman Pratt (1824–1920)	59
The Pink House	60
Tarleton Cadwallader Luce	62

Contents

Chapter Four
The Great Hotels: 1871–79 64
    Highland House Hotel 64
    Sea View House 65
    Prospect House 68
    The Wesley House 68
1874 69
    Illumination and Fireworks 70
    Presidential Visit 70
    Killing and Murder in the News 71
Agassiz Hall: The Martha's Vineyard Summer Institute 73
Cottage City Star 74

Chapter Five
Freedom 76
Secession: 1880 77
Black Citizens 78
Rural Improvement Society: 1881 80
Town Hall: 1882 81
Phoebe Moseley Adams Ballou: 1883 82
Eunice C. Rocker 83
The Flying Horses: 1884 84
Electricity 85
Soldiers' Memorial Fountain: Charles Strahan
    (November 10, 1840–March 24, 1931) 85
    Reconciliation, Redemption and Repudiation 85
Titticut Follies 88

Chapter Six
The Oakland Mission: 1895 89
The Bradley Memorial Church 90
Portuguese American Club 91
The Woman in Red 92
The Automobile Arrives 93
Phillip J. Allston (1860–1915) 96
Shearer Cottage 97
Dorothy West 97
The Inkwell 99
Golf 101

Contents

The Phidelah Rice School for the Spoken Word	103
The Arcade: Blind Nathan	105

Chapter Seven
Diversions	107
The Tivoli Ballroom	108
Dreamland	109
Movie Theaters	111
The Herald and the Old Variety Store	112
Henry (Harry) Thacker Burleigh (December 2, 1866–September 12, 1949)	114
Airplanes: "$10.00 for 10 Minutes"	116
Prohibition	117
Stuart MacMackin	117
Eben Davis Bodfish	118
Phyllis Clair Deitz (September 2, 1921–July 22, 2014)	119
Reverend Leroy C. Perry (1874–June 26, 1960)	120

Chapter Eight
Joseph Sequeira Vera (July 14, 1928–May 22, 2018)	122
Joseph August Sylvia (August 19, 1892–December 2, 1968)	124
Adam Clayton Powell Jr. (November 29, 1908–April 4, 1972)	125
Johnny Seaview	127
Charles H. "Cee Jay" Jones	128
Black Resort	129
Dr. Adelaide M. Cromwell	130
The Swanson House: William Melvin Davey	130
Coleman's Corner	131
The Swanson House Redux: Truman R. Gibson Jr.	132
Herbert Loring Jackson (1908–1978)	132
Cottagers Corner	133
Judge Herbert Edward Tucker (August 30, 1915–March 1, 2007)	134
Lenwood Joseph Overton	135
Rally at the Tabernacle	136

Chapter Nine
The *Delegate*: C. Melvin Patrick	137
Lincoln G. Pope Jr. (May 29, 1916–January 10, 1979)	138
Edward W. Brooke (October 26, 1919–January 3, 2015)	139

Contents

Lucy Hart Abbot	142
Cilian B. Powell and James L. Hicks	144
Dr. Kenneth C. Edelin (March 31, 1939–December 30, 2014)	146
Justine Tyrell Priestly Smadbeck (1921–2004)	147
Linda Marinelli (February 27, 1931–January 31, 2013)	149

Chapter Ten

Lola's	152
Clarence Leroy Holte (February 19, 1909–January 29, 1993)	154
Signs of Oak Bluffs	154
Della Louise Brown Taylor Hardman (May 20, 1922–December 13, 2005)	155
Wayne Coutinho (August 15, 1946–June 3, 2002)	155
Coin Diving	157
Chief Eric Blake	158
African Americans at Home on an Island	158

Chapter Eleven

Philip H. Reed (February 21, 1949–November 6, 2008)	159
The Bolling Family	160
The Nelson Family	161
Final Thoughts	161
Notes	163
Bibliography	173
About the Author	176

ACKNOWLEDGEMENTS

Along with the people and characters included in this book, I owe much to many, including Jane Seagrave, the publisher of the *Vineyard Gazette* who hired me to write the Oak Bluffs town column; her husband, John Kennedy, who encouraged me to write (and edited my book about whale captains of color); and Julia Wells, editor of the *Vineyard Gazette*, who edited and improved my columns and commentaries. Hilary Wall, the *Vineyard Gazette*'s librarian, and Dr. A. Bowdoin "Bow" Van Riper, Martha's Vineyard Museum research librarian, were both incredibly helpful in providing me with access to articles and images. Christopher Rowan, historian, writer and friend from Eastville, supplied me with quite a bit of information on the historical Eastville community and characters, particularly the Luce family.

Thank you to the many readers of the 253 columns I wrote for the *Vineyard Gazette* from 2012 to 2017.

Most thanks though go to Karen W. Finley, a personal cheerleader and my adopted angel, who consistently reminds me I can do what I'm pretty sure I can't.

Oak Bluffs? It's a place where you don't have to catch your breath.

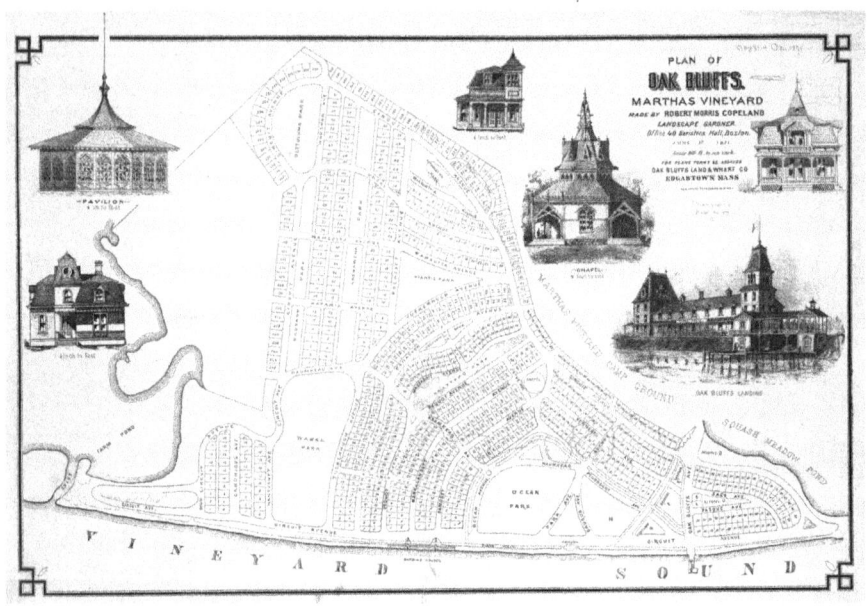

Plan of Oak Bluffs by Robert Morris Copeland. *Courtesy of the Norman B. Leventhal Map & Education Center at the Boston Public Library.*

INTRODUCTION

The history of one's own locality should be known to each of its citizens, since one cannot appreciate the present conditions without some understanding of the causes which have produced these conditions.

—*Henry Franklin Norton*
Martha's Vineyard: History, Legends, Stories

Henry Franklin Norton was born in Oak Bluffs in 1888. From 1949 to 1961, he was curator of the Dukes County Historical Society and generously included black and original people in his work. From 2012 to 2017, my weekly *Vineyard Gazette* column, Town of Oak Bluffs, included history because I love our town and thought it might be interesting. Oak Bluffs' history is available in several publications but not necessarily in any chronological order. Our roots officially began with the Methodists in 1835. This book curates my column to trace highlights of Oak Bluffs' unique history in an effort to portray a welcoming resort community with an atypically diverse group of people.

Anne Simon offers a description about Martha's Vineyard's people in her book *No Island Is an Island*:

> *This variety attracts an extraordinary mix of citizens to the Vineyard. One of Massachusetts' two Indian towns is at the west end of the island, one of America's first and most exclusive yacht clubs at the east, and in between,*

INTRODUCTION

a community frequently cited as the only middle-class black seaside resort on the East Coast....There are descendants of Portuguese pioneers who came from the Azores and Cape Verde Islands on whale ships. There are new Vineyarders who have migrated to start a business or to retire in one of the three more urban down-island towns, there are New Englanders whose ancestors were the first white settlers here, whalers, fishermen, farmers, whose names still dominate up-island villages as well as the streets and stores of the towns.

I hope you'll enjoy these stories of Oak Bluffs, which begin with mine.

CHAPTER ONE

Vineyard historical writer David McCullough pointed out that "history is who we are and why we are the way we are" in his commencement address to Wesleyan University's class of 1984.

My Story

In June 1955, the automobile trip from Long Island, New York, to Oak Bluffs, Martha's Vineyard, was a journey. There was not only no Route 195, there was no Route 95, so the trip was almost wholly along the serpentine, stop-light-speckled Route 1. Today's four-hour, 250-mile drive was then an arduous nine to ten hours in Dad's Pontiac station wagon crammed with a season's worth of clothes and supplies—and it was tortuous for the parents of three kids all under the age of reason. Due to circumstance and with Dad's overabundance of caution, there were only two stops for gas and the bathroom. The Ewell and Millie Finley family first came to Oak Bluffs with the Desi and Ann Margetson family (with two youngsters of their own) and shared a small house on Dukes County Avenue that first summer.[2]

Ann Margetson
(December 28, 1931–April 20, 2014)

When the Oak Bluffs Land Wharf Company built what became the town's historic district, the homes, hotels and buildings were constructed of wood—

Ann Margetson at Menemsha, 1965. *Courtesy of Neil Margetson.*

perhaps, as my father suggested, out of loblolly pine, a fast-growing tree grown throughout the southeast coast. Clay from the old brickyard in Menemsha was used for bricks. The process required heat, generated by burning wood. The yard operated from the mid-1700s to 1930, when the consumption of both wood and clay proved unsustainable. As a result, my family home is one of only a few with a brick basement in the Cottage City Historic District. When my folks bought the house during our first summer in 1955, they said the climate would help my allergies and asthma. This was before we recognized things like attention deficit disorders—before realizing that giving children antihistamines was the equivalent of dosing them with speed—and I wasn't the best kid anyway. The true story, though, was that we came the first time as two families. The dads were both engineers and the moms were stay-at-homes with young ones. Both modern moms believed that Dr. Spock's *Baby and Child Care* was the kid instruction manual, and the more liberal of the two mothers was Ann Margetson, whose idea it had been to share a summer vacation in Oak Bluffs. My sister Debbie, my brother Glenn, and the Margetson sons, Neil and Evan, have stories, too, but I got to write mine. Ann Margetson wasn't black like the rest of us and her husband, Desi. She was white, but back then, we children didn't know that was a big deal. We knew the tiny house on Dukes County Avenue was where we were forced to sleep (Neil didn't like sleeping) and play games on rainy days (Glenn didn't play well with others). We all liked peanut butter and jelly and tuna sandwiches (I still do) at the beach called the Inkwell, where we stayed in the water from 10:00 a.m. to 6:00 p.m. or until we turned purple and wrinkly. I didn't like leaving the water, and when I got cranky, it was usually Ann who would take me for a walk on the beach. Her quiet voice calmed me down, and while talking about my behavior, she would stop for us to discover beach glass and, mysteriously enough, parts of bricks worn smooth like beach glass. Over the years, I managed to find two whole bricks, one newish and the other weathered and bearing the name Sage. They were the first things I thought of when Evan told me his mom had died. It turns out that the prized bricks and pieces we found were probably made on Fisher Island, between the Connecticut and Long Island shorelines, by DeWitt Clinton Sage's Fisher Island Brick Manufacturing Company. Many municipal buildings in Massachusetts—and maybe some here—used Sage bricks. The hurricane of 1938 conspired to close the company, making it imaginable that Sage bricks on our shores may have had the assistance of nature in getting here. I still have those bricks and a bunch of beach glass collected since the days when Aunt Ann showed me how to find them. Ann Margetson was also an artist. She built the walkway at her house on Wamsutta Avenue with bricks she found at the Inkwell. They remain, enhanced with the patina of moss. Born in New York City, she died peacefully in her lifelong home on Easter Sunday. I'm grateful for the memories, but I'll miss Ann, especially on those days when I'm searching for beach glass—and brick parts.[3]

On October 15, 1872, the Oak Bluffs Land and Wharf Company sold 18 Pequot Avenue to William H. Hart of New Britain, Connecticut, for $125. Hart was the president of Stanley Tool Works and founder of today's Hart Haven neighborhood. Another hardware magnate, manufacturer Philip Corbin, built a home on Ocean Park (the Norton House). It is easy to imagine

(Left to right) Neil Margetson, Glenn Finley, Evan Margetson, Deborah Finley and Skip Finley. The modified Claflin Cottage is in background at top right. *Author's Collection.*

that Corbin's hardware, including hooks, fasteners, locks and knobs, and Stanley tools were used in the construction of Oak Bluffs. Coincidentally, the companies today are combined as Stanley Black & Decker.[4]

Ours is the fifth family to own the house and the fourth to live in it. Dad bought it from his lawyer, Henry Corey, who never lived in it. For over sixty years, family tradition has allowed our kids to go to town unaccompanied at night. "Town" of course was Circuit Avenue, with different curfews as time went on. They started at 9:00 p.m. but gradually extended to 10:00 and 11:00 by the time we were fifteen or sixteen. We picked up mail from the post office and used the laundry where Offshore Ale is today. We brought jelly donuts home from the Old Stone Bakery and milk, bread and eggs from the Reliable Grocery Store. We picked up hardware from Phillips while the dads worked on weekend fixit projects. Freedom to roam Circuit Avenue at night taught us how to interact with adults, handle money and develop self-respect without fear. We stayed with the moms all summer long, the dads returning on the last ferries—the "Daddy boat"—on Friday and Sunday nights.

This was a privileged way to grow up.

Foundations

The Pleistocene Epoch or Ice Age lasted from about 2.6 million years ago until 9600 BC, when the ice receded, separating Martha's Vineyard from the mainland. With some irony and an Oak Bluffs relationship, Louis Agassiz is credited with the initial theories of the Ice Age as published in his 1840 book, *Études sur les glaciers* (*Studies on Glaciers*). Edward Hitchcock's work *The Geology of Massachusetts* in 1841 substantiated Agassiz and essentially proved how the island's and specifically Oak Bluffs' topography was formed.[5]

The glacier wended its way across land and receded, created an outwash plain when it melted. Its withdrawal left behind a terminal moraine, the detritus pushed by the front edge of the ice that made the land. The combination of glacial movement, wind and weather provided our sand, soil, streams, ponds and rocks, established our climate and formed what the indigenous people called Ogkeshkuppe or "the wet (or damp) woods,"[6] which we named Oak Bluffs. The paucity of land is such that everything counts for inspection or introspection. When the glacier left us with the scant land comprising Ogkeshkuppe, huge blocks of ice were buried in the outwash plain. Insulated by the ground, they melted more slowly and left deep impressions on the surface like Dodger's Hole, which is called a kettle hole. Little Pond, in the forest, is another of these, and there are more in the trails of the Southern Woodlands.[7]

In a review of David R. Foster's book *A Meeting of Land and Sea: Nature and the Future of Martha's Vineyard* (*Vineyard Gazette*, December 22, 2016), Tom Dunlop wrote, "Thanks to a glacier, Martha's Vineyard was the last piece of ground to be created in all of New England. Thanks to the rising sea, it will be the first to go."

Discovery

In AD 1000, Viking Leif Ericsson named the island Vineland. In 1006, Icelander Thorfinn Karlsefne recounted his sailing voyage to an island with strong currents around it that he named Straumey in Icelandic or "Stream Island."[8]

The Native Americans called it Nope—"amid the waters." Historian Dr. Charles Banks reinterpreted it as Noepe. Despite being inhabited by three thousand indigenous people, in 1602, England's Bartholomew Gosnold sailed to and around the Elizabethan Islands on the *Concord*, "discovering" and renaming Noepe Martha's Vineyard in honor of our grapes and his mother—or daughter or wife as one chooses to believe.[9]

Gosnold established a small post at neighboring Cuttyhunk Island in 1602. Had the colony stayed settled, it would have been the oldest in British America, before Jamestown (1607) and the Pilgrims (1620). Ironically, although Gosnold decided not to stay on Cuttyhunk, he became one of three captains to land at Jamestown on May 13, 1607—he died (and is buried) there four months later.[10]

Contact

Oak Bluffs belonged to who I like to call the original people.

They were the Nunnepog sachemship (or tribe) of the Wampanoag Nation. For centuries, they fished and farmed and founded a benign and mutually beneficial culture that was a tad male dominant but where women wound up doing most of the work. In 1613, some English sea captains, including John Smith, decided to take hostages back to England, one of who was a Nunnepog named Epanow. During the year of his captivity, he learned the English would do anything for gold, including returning him to his home to find some. Returning in 1614, Epanow made his escape with the help of twenty canoes filled with friends and relatives the bamboozled English were led to believe had come to trade for gold. In 1621, Captain Thomas Dermer, an earlier visitor, landed at Nunnepog with his crew, who were "set upon," and many were killed. Dermer never recovered from his own wounds. Remarkably, that was the only time the indigenous people and the white immigrants clashed in the history of the island—not counting the disease brought inadvertently that ultimately killed off 90 percent of an estimated 3,000 of them. By the time of a census taken in 1764, there were only 313 native people left.[11]

Meanwhile, over in Plymouth after the *Mayflower*'s arrival, the one written account of the first Thanksgiving by participant Edward Winslow, in his letter published in 1622, described the three-day event, noting the harvest of corn and barley with a few peas, wild turkey and five deer King Massasoit and his ninety men contributed. Winslow didn't mention that the *Mayflower*'s trip around the cape included the desecration of graves, looting corn, beans and other stores as the Pilgrims found their way to the home they would ultimately adopt.[12]

Of the 102 passengers and 50 crewmen that left England, 53 were left alive in March 1621 to build huts ashore. The Natives steered the newcomers to the local food of clams, mussels, lobster, eel, ground nuts, acorns, walnuts, chestnuts, squash and beans and strawberries, raspberries, grapes and gooseberries. Once a whale ship before bringing the Pilgrims, the *Mayflower* went on to Greenland to continue participating in the decimation of the whales for food, oil and manufacturing material.[13]

The indigenous people, from whom we learned whaling, had pursued it before 1605. The Pilgrims tried almost immediately, and commercial whaling began on Martha's Vineyard in 1738, when Captain John Chase sailed out on the *Diamond*.[14]

Along with Nantucket, New Bedford and, to an extent, Sag Harbor, we became an integral part of what was the time's Middle East—but for a different type of oil. The best harpooners and captains came from Martha's Vineyard, and Edgartown bloomed with the trappings of wealth still evident today, even after more than 350 years.

But it didn't last.

New Religion

Governor Thomas Mayhew

Born in 1593 and once an apprentice merchant from Southampton, Thomas Mayhew immigrated to Medford, Massachusetts, in 1631. In October 1641, he purchased Martha's Vineyard, Nantucket and the Elizabeth Islands and became their governor. Mayhew sent his son Thomas with a few families to colonize it and minister to the Indians. In 1642, the governor brought more settlers and supplies, and he stayed until he died in 1682 at the age of eighty-nine.[15]

Thomas Mayhew is believed to have been President George W. Bush's tenth great-grandfather.[16]

The new homeland was called Great Harbor Township until Governor Mayhew changed it to Edgartown.

Thomas Mayhew Jr. and Hiacoomes

Thomas Mayhew Jr. was the first to convert a Native person when, in 1648, he convinced Hiacoomes to adopt the Christian religion. This earned Oak Bluffs a place in the history of colonialism. Hiacoomes is believed to have been born in 1620. Described as having a mean (serious) countenance and slow speech, he was amenable to meeting with the English thanks to Mayhew's encouragement. Mayhew, quick to learn the Algonquin/Wampanoag language, found Hiacoomes willing, and the two developed a trust that led to a relationship of teacher and student of religion. Following the English settlement in 1643, several members of the tribe got sick, and many felt it was due to Hiacoomes and others falling for the ways of the English. Of course we later learned it was due to the diseases the immigrants brought with them, but with his new beliefs and despite the friction, Hiacoomes became a Christian and proceeded to spread the religion. In 1646, Tawanquatuck, one of the island's chief sachems, asked Hiacoomes and Mayhew to speak to him and others, with the result of more credibility for Christianity. In 1650, Hiacoomes lost his wife and a child to disease, and Thomas Mayhew spoke at their funeral. In a letter dated 1650, Mayhew wrote about Hiacoomes: "I must give him this testimony after some years' experience, that he is a man of a sober spirit, and good conversation; and as he hath, as I hope, received the Lord Jesus in truth, so I look upon him to be faithful, diligent, and constant in the work of the Lord, for the good of his own soul and his neighbors with him."

The two had become friends. Another reverend, Henry Whitefield, made a ten-day stop on the Vineyard on a trip from Boston to England interrupted by weather and, having heard of the convert, met and spoke with him. He reported, "I desired to speak with him who preaches to the Indians twice every Lord's day, whose name is Hiacoomes; he is of prompt understanding, of a sober and moderate spirit, and well reported of both by English and Indians."

Tragically, Thomas Mayhew Jr. was lost on a ship traveling back to England in 1657. Hiacoomes continued his preaching until 1683, when he passed the mantle due to old age, and he died in 1690, probably at 70 years old.[17]

In an October 16, 1651 letter Thomas Mayhew wrote to Reverend Henry Whitefield, he described the location of Hiacoomes's teaching: "Where stood the rock on a descending ground upon which he used to sometimes stand and preach."[18]

Pulpit Rock

Pulpit Rock was where Mayhew preached to the Native Americans, including Hiacoomes. There are a few possible locations of Pulpit Rock that are actually boulders. From County Road, east down Pulpit Rock Road, one comes to a split. The right fork, about a mile down, ends at the Land Bank's Pecoy Point Preserve; the left split goes to the private Norton Cemetery in Waterview Farms. Originally the neighborhood was called Pohqu-auk, meaning "open land," by its inhabitants. Most of this part of Oak Bluffs—from Sengekontacket and almost all the way over to the Lagoon—was treeless, rolling meadows. This special place was used for gathering shell fish and eels and growing corn, squash and tobacco, and it was a Native settlement. Some evidence supports that the rock is located on the way to Pecoy Point on the left amid a stand of trees. Another possibility is Norton Cemetery—a boulder in the back of it resembles a pulpit. This is the one I suspect may have been the actual rock, principally because it's closer to the trail system and farther from where I imagine the original people actually lived. Supporting the hallowed nature of the spot, Native American graves are clearly marked with larger stones where the head would be and smaller ones at the feet among the headstones of the cemetery. Both of the possible Pulpit Rocks are erratics—huge, immovable boulders made by bedrock and left by the Ice Age.[19]

Maintaining Pulpit Rock's reverence, years later, a former slave, John Saunders, preached Methodism here to the colored people, black and indigenous. In 1646, Thomas Mayhew called our part of Martha's Vineyard the "Eastermost Chop of Homses Hole," the word "chop" being a variation of "chap," the jaw of a vise or a clamp. Originally called Ogisske by the indigenous people, the name was changed to Farm Neck by Oak Bluffs' first white settler, Joseph Daggett, whose father, John, had come to the island with the Mayhews.[20] He married Ahoma, the beautiful daughter of the sachem (chief) of Sanchakantackett (Sengekontacket), often called "Martha's Vineyards Pocahontas." Isaac Norton sold the land to Daggett on February 13, 1685.[21]

One can hear how Pecoy came from Pohqu-auk phonetically. The main source of fresh water was Weahtaqua ("place of the boundary spring") at the Land Bank's Weahtaqua Springs Preserve at the southernmost point of the Lagoon, where the Oak Bluffs water department pumping station is. The people traversed between these places by way of an ingenious pattern of trails. Pecoy Point is connected with Pulpit Rock Road, which

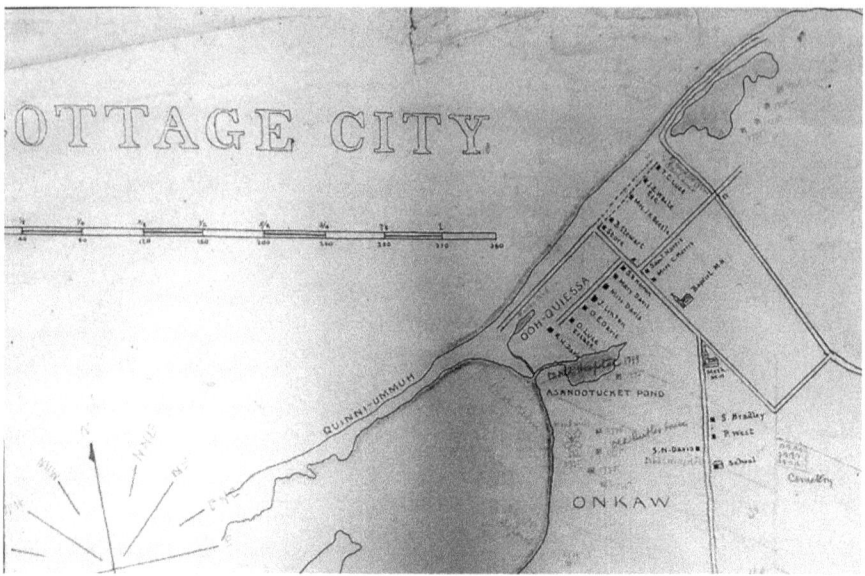

Eastville map. *Courtesy of Christopher Rowan.*

crosses County Road at one of the entrances to Meadow View Farm. The Chase Road begins here before intersecting with the Cross Oak Bluffs Trail, which extends south to Holmes Hole Road and across Barnes Road to Weahtaqua. The trail systems have been adopted as "special ways" and are protected and conserved. While rarely used, you will find they are easily—instinctively—seen on a walk or trail bike ride. With many of our street names being derived from the Algonquin language, one could believe Oak Bluffs was central to the island Wampanoags. As it turns out, we didn't have a large native population during the contact period (when the Europeans came). Ogkeshkuppe was subordinate to the Takemmy and Nunnepog sachems to the south.

While it seems our tiny town has more native names than the others, it was actually white men who provided the appellations. In Algonquin, Tikhoma was the area at the head of the Lagoon, and Quatapog (Quantapog) was a small pond. Quosaquannes was what we now call East Chop. Island-wide, Algonquin named the places and villages along the coast and ponds and estuaries like in Oak Bluffs. Generally, our indigenous ancestors only bothered naming places for what occurred there.[22] Those who came later used names for identification, location or ownership, the lack of understanding of which is why they often tried to kill all the original owners.

Unless you were around when Oak Bluffs was Ogkeshkuppe, you wouldn't be familiar with Quinni-ummuh Street over in Ooh-quiessa near Asanootucket Pond. These names are clearly indicated on an 1850s map of Cottage City but today are Beach Road (Ooh-quiessa) opposite the Martha's Vineyard Hospital alongside Brush (Asanootucket) Pond. This was the area just southwest of Bellevue Heights and directly north of Onkaw, the Lagoon Heights neighborhood. The Wampanoag (or Wôpanâak) version of the Algonquin language is virtually extinct. It was the first Native American language to develop and use an alphabetic writing system due to the early missionaries who used it to convert the Wampanoag to Christianity. Today, thanks to efforts by members of the Assonet, Mashpee, Herring Pond and Aquinnah Wampanoags, there are substantive efforts to reclaim a language that hasn't had any fluent speakers for over 150 years. The Wôpanâak Language Reclamation Project was started in 1993 by Jessie Little Doe Baird, who earned a master's in Algonquian linguistics in 2000. There is a child now being raised with Wampanoag as a first language as part of this project.[23]

One reason to reclaim the indigenous Wampanoag language might be…suppose Quinni-ummuh meant "Where we hid the gold." Another might be to gain a better understanding of the history of the stewards of the land who came before us, like the Niantics, members of a First Nation with a sad story. By 1870, they were declared extinct, but they live in memory here in Oak Bluffs thanks to the tennis, basketball and children's park formed by Wamsutta, Tuckernuck and Pocasset Avenues. A citizens group designed and built a space reflecting the character of Oak Bluffs on a scale appropriate for a family playground with privately raised funds and public help from the town.[24]

Niantic Park is one of Oak Bluffs' nine original parks. The tribe originally included about 4,000 people but was reduced to about 1,500 by diseases brought from England. In a complicated story, in 1634, Niantic warriors killed John Stone, who was kidnapping Niantic women and children to sell as slaves in Virginia. In retribution, most of them were killed or sold as slaves in the West Indies. Connecticut declared the tribe extinct in 1870 and sold its three-hundred-acre reservation.[25]

We honor their memory by knowing their story.

Geography and Geology

Looking down at a map or from a plane, Oak Bluffs looks like the mitten of Martha's Vineyard. Our coastline is changing, and it's easier to predict how it will look in the future than guess how it looked when the glaciers formed the island. Most of it was barren, and when the original people first settled here, the topography was remarkably different. The Farm Neck area was flat, protected by marshland inland of Sengekontacket Pond. You could see the Lagoon and Sengekontacket from the hilly crest lining County Road. Those views are now blocked by the oak trees that outgrow everything. North of Farm Neck, at the end of the golf course and around Wing Road was farmland, much of it now also covered by oak trees. We're known for damp thickets rather than forests; our light, quick-draining soil doesn't allow trees to reach the height needed to build an understory beneath their canopies for a forest to develop. Oak withstands the wind and salty air and thrives while other hardwood trees cannot. Over time, it is said, the oaks would cover the entire island.[26] In 1835, we cut them down to build the city in the woods of our Campground.

Oak Bluffs is the biggest little town on Martha's Vineyard, itself the third-largest island on the East Coast. Oak Bluffs consists of 7.14 square miles—4,680 acres (including ponds) 2,157 of which are developed with 3,820 homes, 1,604 of which were occupied year-round (2,216 are seasonal) in 2008.[27] Almost 60 percent of our total homes are summer residences, and as many as 500 historic homes have no heat or insulation.[28] Ranking fifth of the six towns in total area, Oak Bluffs' population is the largest and most diverse, its diversity a large part of its uniqueness. Only because people are the way they are do we have racists—but not (generally) racism. We're Wampanoag, European immigrants, born free and descended from slaves of color, Portuguese, Azorean, Cape Verdean and Brazilian year-round and who knows how many other nationalities and colors during the tourist season. Apocryphally, as many as half the town's homes may be owned by black people. While only 3.4 percent of the year-round population is black, those who live in Oak Bluffs account for 19.6 percent of all 780 who live on Martha's Vineyard (Dukes County) year-round. Census estimates in 2017 indicate that Oak Bluffs has a population of 4,527 persons, 90.4 percent of whom are white. The other 9.6 percent includes 153 who are black, 229 of two or more races, 140 some other race alone, and another 137 Latino, Asian or American Indian (34).[29]

It is commonly accepted that the island has about 130,000 visitors at any given time during its Memorial Day–to–Columbus Day season (1.2 million total), and while there is no adequate estimate, 20,000 (or more) may be African American. With forty-two official and unofficial neighborhoods, 1.3 square miles of the town are composed of water, about 15 percent of its total area. Fittingly—as the only town one can drive from end to end and still see water, whether choosing Cottage City's secession from Edgartown on February 17, 1880, or its January 25, 1907 incorporation as Oak Bluffs, the town is astrologically an Aquarian. It's fitting that the sign for a town that began as a seaside watering place would be the "water bearer."

Oak Bluffs houses and shares the high school, two of five island movie theaters, one of two ferry terminals, one of six lighthouses and two of three bridges, one that opens for nautical traffic. We have an elementary school, a library, a senior citizen center, numerous trails, a bunch of places of worship—indoors and outdoors—a golf course, the carousel, the skating rink, the skate park, the bowling alley, a private airport and the largest marina.

Thanks to our being the home of the hospital, almost everyone not born at home or in an ambulance is born in Oak Bluffs.[30]

We have a roundabout, although there are no traffic lights island-wide. We have 429 homes in the Cottage City Historic District and 315 in the Campground, over 600 of which are included on historic registers. There are 452 well-maintained streets connecting our neighborhoods and providing access to 55 named parks, 17 ponds, 7 cemeteries and 7 beaches, one that we share with Edgartown (Joseph Sylvia State beach) and another shared with Vineyard Haven (Eastville beach).[31]

Steeped in history, Circuit Avenue, our main street, has thirty-six stores and shops, twenty-eight of which are close to if not 100 years old. One, the Arcade, was 152 years old in 2019.

THE BARBARY COAST

Oak Bluffs has earned its prized honky tonk reputation. In the 1700s, our first neighborhood, Edgartown's Eastville/Farm Neck area, was tongue-in-cheekily referred to as the Barbary Coast. One of the main Vineyard docks was located at a road to nowhere at the north end of Eastville Avenue near the site of the famous Eastville Inn, our first tavern. It is said that the Pilgrims on the *Mayflower* brought more beer than water to freedom in the New World, understandable since its alcoholic content made it safer to drink. Along with being an early analgesic, alcohol tended to enhance the quality of life and make hard work easier. So the English heritage of drinking was passed along to its progeny here on the island. Early settlers and visitors eked existences from the sea. Whaling, fishing and shipping were dangerous occupations, so when people made landfall they wanted to eat, drink and be merry as tomorrow was not guaranteed. When "Jack"—as the seamen were referred to—came ashore, the only public houses available were in Eastville. The Eastville Inn was one of several—others were taverns named Claghorn, Cunningham, Cousins, Pease, Davis, Smith and the Linton Tavern, one of Oak Bluffs' oldest homes.[32]

Near the docks, Eastville was where sailors and seamen met when ashore between passages. Beginning in 1730, these inn holders and taverns were licensed by the county to do business, setting the stage for Oak Bluffs' future as the town everyone from performers to presidents wanted to see and be seen in. Crucially for its future, while there were taverns down in Edgartown, Oak Bluffs establishments were oft ignored by our southern betters.

Early Economics

Martha's Vineyard's economy then was one of subsistence, based on agriculture and fishing from its first contact until 1738, when whaling began making Edgartown wealthy. By 1894, Vineyard-based whaleships—not including Edgartown-owned ships that left from other ports—had returned with whale oil and products valued at $228 million today.[33]

In 1776, we were stripped of herds and agricultural products and our whaleships were attacked by the British in the Revolutionary War. Martha's Vineyard's first casualty of the war was Sharper Michael, a former slave whose great-grandson William A. Martin would become a whale captain. Michael was killed in 1777 by a wayward musket ball from the British privateer *Cerberus*.[34]

The attacks on whaling continued in the War of 1812 and the Civil War. By the time the whaling industry came to an end, we were primed to become a vacation resort.

Methodism

In 1787, the former slave John Saunders, with his half-white wife Priscilla, was brought from Virginia by Captain Thomas Luce hidden beneath corn Luce was transporting. Saunders, a preacher, brought Methodism with him forty-eight years before it was established by the Martha's Vineyard Camp Meeting Association and before the Wesleyan Grove settlement established Oak Bluffs' tabernacle grounds. Saunders is remembered via a plaque on a rock on the trail at Pecoy Point Preserve. This spot on the Martha's Vineyard African American Heritage Trail marks his preaching at Pulpit Rock to the "coloured" and original people in the Farm Neck neighborhood. He and his wife lived in Eastville until 1792, when they moved to Chappaquiddick, where she died and where he was later killed by the local Natives after marrying one of their own.

New Beginnings

In 1790, the first U.S. Census counted thirty-nine apparently free black people on Martha's Vineyard, ten of whom lived in Edgartown and the rest in Farm Neck. The neighborhood had about fifteen homes that are estimated to have housed ninety-one people year-round.

On January 23, 1790, signing the deed with his "X," Native American Robert Seaton (an illiterate "Indianman labourer,") sold a parcel of land for ten pounds to Samuel Norton (a descendant of Ichabod Norton, who owned the area where Pulpit Rock is located). Seaton's mark was witnessed by Thomas Cooke, Edgartown's justice of the peace. The deed indicated that the parcel of land was "commonly called and known by the name of Farm Neck."[35]

Later, Samuel Norton's descendant Captain Shubael Lyman Norton would sell part of it to the Oak Bluffs Land and Wharf Company.

Ichabod Norton and Old Harry

Oak Bluffs is enriched by its beloved characters, and two from that neighborhood were "Uncle" Ichabod Norton and his black servant, "Old Harry." Uncle Ichabod was very wealthy and was referred to as the "Bank of Edgartown." Once, after a man's horse died, his petition to Uncle Ichabod for help read, "The Almighty having seen fit to take from this poor man his only beast of burden, we the undersigned are willing to help him secure another." Ichabod refused, because if God decided to take more horses, his entire fortune wouldn't be enough. The man persevered, so finally Ichabod's humorous response in giving him five dollars was, "Seeing that you and the Almighty have been in communication and have come to some understanding, I will help you this time."

Old Harry deserted a ship anchored in Vineyard Haven in 1790 to escape slavery. Calling himself John Harry Monus John Peter Tobirus Peter Toskirus Peter Tubal Cain—Old Harry for short—he became Ichabod Norton's servant. Old Harry was well spoken and apparently well educated, although he never divulged his background. He was once sent on an errand and delivered the message "My mistresses, the Miss Lydia and Miss Martha Norton, send their respects to their cousin Mrs. Rebecca Norton and family, and hope that they find themselves well, and that they can easily lend a little pepper."[36]

I enjoy imagining Old Harry insisting to his "betters" that he wanted to be referred to by his whole name. After fifty years of service to the Nortons, Old Harry received a single silver dollar that he wore around his neck until his death in 1845—when a neighbor stole it. Old Harry is buried at the Norton Cemetery near Pulpit Rock, in Native American fashion, with a rock at the head and a smaller one at the feet of the departed with no marked stone.

I like to stop by Norton Cemetery with a smile for Old Harry—a genius, escaped from slavery, paid to live free and die in Oak Bluffs.

The Azores

Emanuel Joseph is believed to have been the first Portuguese settler on Martha's Vineyard. Born in the Azores in 1774, he married Mehitable Luce here in 1796.[37] Most of the early folks from the Azores were sailors or whalers—thankfully for Oak Bluffs, it was largely due to the Portuguese that the town's year-round population increased. By 1871, an article in a New Bedford newspaper about Cottage City's growth pointed out "men and women of all nations and all natures, of all sections and complexions—the Portuguese, the Englishman, the Frenchman, the Southerner, the Easterner—all going to the Eden-like city by the sea." Once the promising new projects of the future failed, land earmarked for development was sold as farmland and taken advantage of by the Portuguese, who brought farming skills with them.

CHAPTER TWO

In 1830, there were forty-one free black people identified on Martha's Vineyard: twenty in Edgartown (which included Oak Bluffs), twelve in Tisbury and nine in Chilmark.[38]

ABOLITIONISTS

There's no clear beginning of when abolitionism became a widely held practice on Martha's Vineyard. Freedom from slavery in America started on Nantucket in 1773 and came to Massachusetts in 1783. Oak Bluffs was home to several abolitionists who helped set the stage for it to become a Place of Pride—a place black folks who were firsts in America gravitated to in order to be like everyone else.

Jeremiah Pease (April 8, 1792–June 5, 1857)

Jeremiah Pease was religious, possibly to the point of zealotry. A good-looking man, he and his wife raised ten children. In 1835, Pease and Hebron Vincent acquired the land the Methodists called the Campground from William Bradley, a wealthy island merchant and one of six men who would go on to found the Oak Bluffs Land and Wharf Company.[39]

Pease was born, lived, died and was buried on the island, and he spent much of his time in Eastville and Farm Neck. He was the first keeper of the Edgartown lighthouse, a customs officer, cordwainer (shoemaker), farmer (hay, oats and corn), surveyor, bone setter, carpenter, tent builder and chorister. As customs officer, he received commissions from the sale of whale oil. He somehow found time to slaughter hogs, paint, pick blueberries, cut trees, chop firewood, fish and eel. As part of his Methodist ministry, he traveled on horseback or in carriages and walked when necessary to marry people or be with them when they died. He kept an important diary and wrote using expressions like "died a happy death" and "peacefully and triumphant." One senses his warmth and sensitivity, for example, when he wrote of the Chappaquiddick funeral of Betsey Carter, "a pious coloured woman," in 1842. Pease's diary was serially published in the Martha's Vineyard Museum's *Dukes County Intelligencer*. He began each entry with a weather report, a valuable way of providing a peek into the past. His frequent entries involving black people showed his concern but not much differently than when white people were involved. He wrote on August 8 and 9, 1847:

Jeremiah Pease. *Courtesy of the Martha's Vineyard Museum.*

> *Attended meeting at Eastville. Brother Solomon Athearn attended and preached in PM. Sister Celia Johnson...died about 12 o'clock this day, rejoicing in the hope of a happy immortality....Attended the funeral of Celia Johnson....It was a solemn time. A great number attended her funeral. She was esteemed a pious Godly woman for several years Past. It was affecting to behold her aged Mother taking her last look of her departed child, she being the only colored person now living in all the region of what is called Farm Neck, at which place a very large number of indians and coloured people formerly resided.*

In perspective, this was fourteen years before the Civil War began. One day's diary entry ended, "Sinners awakened, Souls Converted. God grant to carry on this work to his own glory." That was a pretty good description of Jeremiah Pease.

Reverend Hebron Vincent (1805–1890)

Reverend Hebron Vincent was anointed "the man who kept the records" of the Camp Meeting Association.[40]

Vincent had no formal education other than part of a year at Maine Wesleyan Seminary. He apprenticed with shoemaker Jeremiah Pease at age thirteen, converted to Methodism at seventeen and received lessons from the "good educated brother" that led to his becoming the Camp Meeting secretary for thirty-five years. His writing about establishing Wesleyan Grove is the only such chronicle of any American camp meeting (there have been several around the country). Hebron Vincent was a self-educated teacher, minister, attorney, historian and community leader. The Martha's Vineyard Museum has Hebron's beautifully penned (but difficult to read) sixteen-and-a-half-page treatise "A Vindication of the African Race" proving his sensitivity to black people. This was unique in the days when most islanders were ambivalent about slavery. Whaling created opportunity for the indigenous people and African Americans in particular, some of whom, like Frederick Douglass (who visited the island), were able to use it to escape from slavery. *Vineyard Gazette* editor and publisher Edgar Marchant deplored the fact that slavery had supplanted so many other economic interests. He wrote on November 27, 1857,

Hebron Vincent. *Courtesy of the Martha's Vineyard Museum.*

> *While upon this subject, it may not be out of place to state that Frederick Douglas* [sic] *the colored gentleman and orator, will lecture before an "Association of gentlemen," at the Town Hall on Saturday evening next. We are not advised as to his subject, but suppose from his antecedents, that he will treat mainly upon the subject of slavery in our country. We hope the learned lecturer will aim more to enlighten his audience than to excite their prejudices against the South; that he will disappoint the expectations of those who can see good in nothing but agitation, by endeavoring to allay rather than excite hatred among the members of the States of the Union. Let peace and concord, and brotherly love, be his watchword, rather than that which leads to strife and all manner of evil. We learn that he will give two lectures next week.*

Obviously Marchant had never been a slave.

There were exceptions to this ambivalence, like Lambert Coves' John Presbury Norton, who petitioned the Massachusetts General Court on February 10, 1849, to be allowed to import slaves to work his farm. The shocked court had the insulting petition withdrawn. In a letter printed by the *Vineyard Gazette* on February 22, 1861, a writer railed against island abolitionists: "We have suffered, too much, the noisy and headstrong to have their own way, and the real state of public sentiment among us, though adverse to slavery, is not of that crotchety character, which a few crack brained enthusiasts, or one-sided men, have exhibited in trying to force themselves to the front rank of anti-slavery movements."

Following Lincoln's inauguration on March 15, 1861, Edgar Marchant began changing his tune, writing in an editorial, "Persuade our people to let slavery alone, wholly and forever, for our meddling, our intemperate speeches, and above all, our pharisaical righteousness, sharing so largely in the profits of slavery, and yet condemning it, has done no good to the slave,—none to the master,—none to the church,—none to the country,—but evil, evil only, and evil continually."

It would be more than another century before African Americans were allowed to purchase homes in the Methodist Campgrounds. Father John F. Wright did preach at the Campground in 1856, and Josiah Henson, a fugitive slave believed to have been the person Harriet Beecher Stowe based Uncle Tom on, preached there in 1858.[41]

While black preachers were allowed to speak and singing groups performed, black people almost never attended—or cared to attend—the meetings.

Robert Morris Copeland

A man with a major role in the development of Oak Bluffs was Robert Morris Copeland, who designed what became the Cottage City Historic District in 1866. He was also a supporter of women's rights. Copeland—an avid abolitionist—tried to develop a training site for a black regiment during the Civil War that ended his career. The appeal for Union support caused his dismissal for insubordination, and his pleas to President Lincoln failing, he moved to Vermont. Copeland recognized that women's issues and slavery were human issues. He is largely credited as being the first person in America to design a residential community.

Robert Copeland died at the age of forty-three in 1873, the year after my family's house on Pequot Avenue was built. I hope he got the chance to see it.

Ebenezer Lamson (1814–1891)

Ebenezer Lamson built a home in the soon-to-fail Bellevue Heights neighborhood in Eastville. He manufactured weapons used by the Union in the Civil War and, like his neighbor Ichabod Norton Luce, was an abolitionist. With his brother and uncle, he started a business in 1837 that grew into the Shelburne, Massachusetts–based company Lamson, Goodnow & Yale, which manufactured scythes and cutlery. They acquired Robbins & Lawrence, a business that built machines to make guns for the Mexican-American War in the 1840s and the Crimean War in the 1850s. When the Civil War started, Lamson went to Washington and got a contract to produce fifty thousand rifles for the Union army. It is believed that the precision instruments made by Lamson, Goodnow & Yale were used by companies that manufactured half of the rifles, muskets, carbines, pistols and bayonets used in the Civil War. In 1869, the company presented President Ulysses S. Grant (who wound up visiting Oak Bluffs five years later) with a sixty-two-piece dinner set. Many of the pieces had ivory handles, and the rest were mother-of-pearl. Some of the pieces are on display at the Smithsonian Institute. Today, Lamson, the oldest cutlery manufacturer in the United States, continues to produce a wide range of knives and kitchen utensils.

Ichabod Norton Luce (1814–1894)

Another notable Farm Neck Norton was Ichabod Norton Luce, born to Silas Luce and Hannah Norton Luce, both of whose families traced their lineage to England in the late 1600s. As a boy, Luce joined the merchant marine business of delivering materials by boat to nearby ports. He went whaling from 1831 to 1838, shipping from New Bedford and Mattapoisett, after which he married Abigail Osborn Fisher of Edgartown. Their son Benjamin was born in Mattapoisett, where Ichabod worked as a boat builder and after meeting and befriending Frederick Douglass became a supporter of the abolitionist movement.[42]

Captaining a whaler again in 1842, in 1848, he joined a company that bought the *Walter Scott,* an old whaler he took to San Francisco during the

Gold Rush. He returned in July 1850 with $3,000 worth of gold—after having sent $5,000 home earlier. Today that gold would be worth over $250,000. Luce opened a grocery store in Vineyard Haven and joined the Edgartown Lyceum, a public lecture hall, where he honed his speaking skills.[43]

In 1853, he was elected president of the Lyceum, and in 1858, he was elected a Massachusetts state senator representing Martha's Vineyard, Nantucket and Cape Cod. During the Civil War, he became keeper of the Gay Head Light, one of the more important aids to navigation

Ichabod Norton Luce. *Courtesy of Christopher Rowan.*

of the time with upwards of ninety thousand boats passing annually. In 1869, he built the Big House, the large white house at the bend of New York Avenue overlooking Vineyard Sound and Vineyard Haven Harbor that the family still owns. Ichabod and his cousin Cad Luce joined the founders of the Dukes County Savings Bank in 1872. Ichabod, a practical man, balked at Edgartown's 1874 investment in the dubious plan for the Martha's Vineyard Railroad, which was built in a mere sixty-six days but was a memory soon after its financial collapse in 1895. Ichabod led the effort to secede from Edgartown, and once we became Cottage City in 1880, he was moderator of our first town meeting. He's buried in the Norton Cemetery at Farm Neck, near Pulpit Rock. The *Vineyard Gazette*'s Henry Beetle Hough wrote about Norton: "Abolitionist, boat builder, mariner, forty-niner, senator, keeper of the Gay Head Light, denouncer of speculative enterprises, divider of a town."

Ichabod Norton Luce contributed a great deal to Oak Bluffs' long-held tolerant attitude.[44]

Edward Dobbs Linton

Edward Dobbs Linton, born in Edgartown in 1814, was a neighbor of Ichabod Norton Luce and Ebenezer G. Lamson. His family owned the Barbary Coast's Linton Tavern in Eastville. Early on, Edward Linton went to New Bedford, apprenticed as a boat builder and became acquainted with

Frederick Douglass, whose ideals he espoused as an editor of the *Liberator*, the abolitionist newspaper founded by William Garrison.[45]

Linton went on to become one of the half-dozen men who founded the Edgartown Lyceum.[46]

Frederick Douglass

Frederick Douglass, the abolitionist and former slave, presented his first Vineyard speech and addressed the nation's values of freedom, Christianity and economic opportunity at the Edgartown Town Hall on Saturday, November 28, 1857, and again spoke at the Federated Church (then known as Congregational Church) the next evening. Edgar Marchant, publisher of the *Vineyard Gazette*, opined in his December 4 editorial:

> *On Sunday evening, he lectured at, to a full house. His subject was slavery, or the slave power in the United States. He failed to handle his subject with the power and ability he displayed in his former lectures, and hence some little disappointment was manifested by the public at the close of the performances. We think Mr. D. is entitled to great respect and to the best wishes of all true lovers of the colored race.*

While nowhere indicated, one wonders if Ichabod Norton Luce or Edward Linton's involvement with the Lyceum had anything to do with Douglass's invitation to the Vineyard.

William Claflin and Hiram Rhodes Revels

William Claflin was an ardent Methodist, abolitionist, liberal and governor of Massachusetts from 1869 to 1872. He served in Congress from 1877 to 1881. In May 1870, Governor Claflin's guest in Boston was Hiram Rhodes Revels, the black man who was appointed as the Confederate Jefferson Davis's replacement as one of the two U.S. senators from Mississippi. Revels spoke at the music hall and visited the Bunker Hill Monument.[47]

Governor Claflin bought a cottage from the Oak Bluffs Land and Wharf Company in 1871 and supported both Indian and female enfranchisement. He and his father contributed funds to buy land for Claflin University, a historically black college in South Carolina that was founded in 1869 and named after his father. Claflin was a significant supporter of higher education for women, signing charters for Wellesley and Mount Holyoke, both women's colleges, as governor.

Gilbert Haven

Gilbert Haven, of 10 Clinton Avenue in Oak Bluffs' Campgrounds, was an "unflinching" anti-segregationist who, in 1873, rode a Mississippi train coach reserved for "coloreds" among other protests. Haven was a Methodist Episcopal pastor and one of the most outspoken U.S. abolitionists of the late 1800s, when the Methodist Episcopal Church tended to support the colonization movement, taking free African Americans and repatriating them to Africa. Bishop Gilbert Haven was one of very few who argued not just to end slavery but also to fully socially integrate African Americans.[48]

In 1874, when President Ulysses S. Grant came to Oak Bluffs, he was the bishop's guest and attended his sermon on Sunday.

These notable abolitionists exerted positive and disproportionate influence over the small populace; there were only 150 people living in Oak Bluffs. Perhaps they were enough to have paved the way for the sense of freedom and tolerance the town has exhibited for the whole of its existence.

Gilbert Haven.
Courtesy of the Martha's Vineyard Museum.

City in the Woods: Prayers for All

The Squash Meadow acquisition by the Camp Meeting Association set the stage for our discovery. Folks heard of the pleasant climate of the small area surrounded by water with gentle breezes during hot summers, and by 1858, there were 320 tents and 12,000 souls attending services, enough so that the nickname "Canvas City" became popular. The fervor of religion met well with a summertime locale. In 1840, a Methodist church was built on Eastville Avenue, followed by a small Baptist church in 1845. After hosting a first camp meeting in 1875 at Highlands Circle, the Baptist Vineyard Association built a permanent wooden octagonal tabernacle of its own in 1878, the same year Trinity Church in the Campgrounds was built for year-round residents. For many years, the Baptists cooperated and held their August meetings the week before the Methodists.

The Baptists welcomed black Vineyarders, which is how the surrounding area of the Highlands later became home to many. Languishing for about ten years, the tabernacle structure received little use, and the grounds were sold to the Highland Property Trust, a group of East Chop residents. Today, the quasi-sacred grounds of Baptist Temple Park remain a natural sanctuary for the neighborhood. The Baptists also built a church on the corner of Pequot and Grove Avenues in 1878, and much of the $3,000 construction cost was afforded by the Camp Meeting Association. The Roman Catholic Church of the Sacred Heart on School Street was built in 1880, and Trinity Episcopalian Church was constructed in 1882. A Seventh-day Adventist church was built on New York Avenue in 1927 and a Christian Scientist church in 1928. Churches continue to play an extraordinary role in Oak Bluffs (and Martha's Vineyard) society today.

Oak Bluffs' legacy as a religious retreat is comfortably diverse choices of religion—highlighted by a modern service at Union Chapel on July 12, 2015, when Rabbi Caryn Broitman (Jewish), Dr. Sarah Sayeed (Muslim) and Reverend Deborah E. Finley-Jackson (AME, my kid sister) shared the pulpit for a service.

The Captains of Cottage City: 1866–74

The Captains who dominated the summer resort development of the past century had much in common, although they were as different as the planets. They were individualists, accustomed to command, and with a strong passion for persons and things which they regarded as their own. To them there was no sharp dividing line between adventure and business....It is impossible to imagine what the course of events on the Island would have been if it had not been for the captains and the promoters.

—*Henry Beetle Hough*

The whaling industry was coming to an end. Island businessmen and whaling captains were looking for new opportunities that ultimately put Oak Bluffs (literally) on the map and the road to fame.[49] The Oak Bluffs Land and Wharf Company (OBLWC) announced its vision in a *Vineyard Gazette* advertisement on July 5, 1867, which read:

> *Home by the Seaside:*
> *"Oak Bluffs"*
> *A new summer resort*
> *One thousand lots for sale laid out by Robert Morris Copeland, Esq., of Boston,*
> *the well-known landscape gardener. Cheap and quiet homes by the sea shore during the summer months. Plans available for beautiful cottages, costing from $300 to $1000*

The company had already begun to build its namesake development on seventy-five acres it had acquired in northeastern Edgartown. The development, a highly speculative scheme, took about six years (1866–72) to conceive and build. It took another ten for the company to self-immolate.

There were far more reasons for the town not to have been built than for its success, for which six men were responsible, led by businessman Erastus P. Carpenter: William S. Hills, William Bradley, Captain Grafton Norton Collins, Captain Ira Darrow and Captain Shubael Lyman Norton, former owner of the land.

Island-born Norton, Collins and Bradley were scions of wealthy families who had taken their inheritances and become richer on their own. Norton, seeking to multiply his gain from the sale of his land with a follow-on investment, reflected the business sense that had brought them success. Darrow had come to the island and become wealthy partly due to his entrepreneurial abilities and partly due to his political leanings, which were mirrored by many in Edgartown. Carpenter and Hills were new to the island—summer visitors with simpler motives. They loved it so much they wanted to build homes as trophies of their success. All of these men were visionaries—men of ego and ambition for whom failure wasn't a consideration. These were leaders accustomed to using their social and political appetites to meet their personal goals.

THE PARTNERS

William Bradley (1825–1895)

William Bradley owned tracts of farmland in the distant northern reaches of Edgartown, including the sheep pasture that, thanks to Jeremiah Pease and Hebron Vincent, in 1835 had become the Methodist Campground. An unnamed, undated newspaper article (probably from the *Vineyard Gazette*) indicated that he arrived at his home on Trinity Park in the Campground in "precarious health" and died soon afterward at the age of seventy.

Captain Shubael Lyman Norton

Shubael Lyman Norton. *Courtesy of the Martha's Vineyard Museum.*

Born near the site where Union Chapel would be built, Shubael Lyman Norton followed his father (also named Shubael) to sea but on merchant ships—a far safer occupation than his father's trade of whaling. He became captain of his own ship in 1852 and remained at sea until 1865, expanding his fortune with voyages to ports in India, China and Australia. He married Phebe A. Davis of Edgartown in 1849, and the two raised a family of three daughters.

It was Norton's idea to divide up his own land into salable lots and turn it into a summer resort, and Norton was president of the company for its first two years (1866–68). The document recording the transfer of the land from the Norton family to the company on June 22, 1870, records the sale price as $1,613.40 (nearly $27,000 today). The couple built their own home on Hartford Park, the long strip of green space bordered by Pequot and Massasoit Avenues.

Norton remained the company's principal agent until 1880 and sold more than half of the thousand lots that the company offered for sale. He died in 1901 at the age of seventy-six and is hailed as the "Father of Oak Bluffs."

Grafton Norton Collins (1820–1889)

Captain Grafton Norton Collins was born in Edgartown at the beginning of the whaling era and after serving as mate in his twenties became a captain at thirty-two. He commanded the whaling ship *Walter Scott* after Luce on back-to-back voyages to the North Pacific from 1852 to 1855 and again from 1855 to 1859. The profits from his whaling were the equivalent of $1.3 million today, and his share would have been roughly $120,000. He married Averick H. Norton in 1860, and in 1862, his uncle died with no family of his own, making Collins heir to his fortune and business interests: whaleships, wharves and companies on the island and the mainland. When the OBLWC was formed, Collins became its first treasurer, and his summer house was one of the earliest built in the Oak Bluffs development.

Ira Darrow (1799–1871)

Ira Darrow was born in Waterford, Connecticut. The master of a fishing vessel, he came to the island in 1825, married Martha Wyer Norton of Nantucket in 1828, and began operating a packet ship—a vessel carrying passengers and freight over a defined route on a more or less regular schedule—between New Bedford and Edgartown. He was appointed master of the Nantucket lightship, owned Darrow's Wharf and went on to hold a series of municipal offices.

Darrow was deeply involved in national politics, often on the wrong side of history. The Vineyard, like the nation, split into four factions during the bitterly contested election of Abraham Lincoln in 1860. Republicans outnumbered Democrats on the island, and Darrow's leadership of the local Democratic faction supported proslavery candidate John Breckenridge.

Gazette editor Edgar Marchant, aligned with the Northern Democrats, declared Darrow, leader of the Southern Democrats, "a smart, enterprising, energetic man and will doubtless make a good and faithful officer" and supported his appointment as customs collector, a position he lost after Abraham Lincoln—who won 59 percent of the vote island-wide and 62 percent in Edgartown—took office in March 1861. He was replaced by Jeremiah Pease's son Jeremiah Jr. Soon after publishing the first issue of the *Vineyard Gazette* on May 14, 1846, Marchant began promoting the island as the "Watering Place" of the East Coast. Darrow became one of the first to work toward implementing Marchant's prediction when, in 1851, he erected a "commodious bathing house… opened for the accommodation of the public" on Edgartown Harbor. Darrow also partnered with Shubael Lyman Norton to build bathhouses on the oceanfront in Oak Bluffs at today's Inkwell beach. Darrow died in 1871, leaving his wife and children twenty shares of the Martha's Vineyard National Bank (of which he had been a director since its founding in 1855), a $10,000 interest in the Oak Bluffs Land and Wharf Company, half-interest in a store in Edgartown, half-interest in each of three ships, a cottage on the Campground and the family home in Edgartown. Altogether, the value of the estate may have been worth over $500,000 today. He lived to see his and his partners' dream of a summer resort come to pass, to participate in its financing and construction and to enjoy a touch of its early success, but he was gone before the beginning of the long downward spiral of its financial demise.

The Off-Islanders: E.P. Carpenter and William Hills

The four Islanders might never have pooled their resources to start a company if it wasn't for E.P. Carpenter and William Hills, summer visitors from the mainland who came to the Vineyard and saw its potential.

Erastus Payson Carpenter was born in Foxboro in 1832. When he came to the Vineyard in 1864 for the Methodist camp meetings in Wesleyan Grove, his own business achievements were already impressive. He had built one of the world's largest straw manufacturing companies and served in various political offices in his hometown.

Delighted by the island, Carpenter wanted to build a cottage in the Campground, but according to the rules of the newly formed Camp Meeting Association, he could only lease a lot—a fact that remains true today. Carpenter built a home on Ocean Park that, completed in 1868 at a cost of $12,000, is assessed today for over $1.5 million. That's not its only story.

Carpenter's friend William Hills made his fortune with his brother Joel at Hills & Brother, a firm that sold its own flour as well as others' on commission. Together, they conceived of the idea for the OBLWC, inviting Bradley, Norton, Collins and Darrow to join the enterprise, bringing their capital (and, in Norton's case, his land) with them.

Triumph, Disaster and Secession

The partners' total investment in the new resort was about $300,000. They spent money quickly and aggressively, creating roads, parks and public buildings. Several of the latter—like Union Chapel and the Arcade building—still remain. The landmark Sea View House hotel, however, lasted only twenty years.

Structure	Cost	Year
The Land	$3,000	1866
The Wharf	$5,000	1867
The Arcade	$6,000	1867
Union Chapel	$16,000	1871
Sea View House	$132,000	1872

They hired Robert Morris Copeland, a cemetery designer from Boston, to draw up the plans. In a move that would later prove controversial but is viewed as prescient today, Carpenter insisted that the company expand the number of parks.

The village of Riverside, Illinois, designed in 1869 by Calvert Vaux and Frederick Law Olmsted, is often claimed to be the first planned community, but the development of Oak Bluffs preceded it due in large part to Carpenter's vision and determination.

Early Oak Bluffs blossomed, its growth geometric as middle-class people from Massachusetts and other parts of the Northeast discovered the pleasant new seaside watering place with its wonderful summer climate and quaint, picturesque homes. However, the company's business model, based on lot sales, proved unsustainable and quickly unraveled.

A balance sheet from October 1872 shows the total outlay to date as $279,955.19. That figure, however, was heavily discounted through depreciation. The aggressive depreciation of the company's assets was designed to hide its most glaring financial problem: it had only 183 lots remaining for sale, virtually no cash on hand and a total debt obligation of nearly $62,000.

In the cold light of day, there were not enough unsold lots remaining to generate the funds required to extinguish the debt. The financial crisis known as the Panic of 1873 and President Ulysses S. Grant's response—contracting the money supply and raising interest rates—made matters even worse for those in debt. The nearby Bellevue Heights development went bankrupt, along with most of the seventeen others that speculators had established in the wake of the OBLWC. The company itself would barely make it into the 1880s.

Katama and the Railroad

Oak Bluffs and its nearby developments, like Wesleyan Grove and Vineyard Highlands, were still part of Edgartown, which, suffering from the collapse of the whaling industry, greedily sought to capture some of the cash being lavished on summer homes in the northernmost part of its town by creating a new resort community in the southernmost part on the sandy plains beside Katama Bay. Captain Nathan Jernegan, who had lost a substantial amount of money when the Dukes County Shoe and Boot Company failed in 1861, founded the Katama Land Company in 1872. He enlisted his close friend and fellow whaling captain Grafton Collins, along with Erastus Carpenter and Joel Hills (the "Brother" of the Hills & Brother flour company). Carpenter was selected as chairman of the new company, Hills became secretary and Robert Morris Copeland was again hired to lay out the new plan for the development. As in Oak Bluffs, a newly built wharf with an elaborate hotel at its head was intended to serve as a formal entryway to the development. Visitors would arrive by ship, pass through an archway at the center of the hotel and emerge into a mosaic of house lots beyond. The hotel was completed at the end of the 1873 season, but it became readily apparent that boat transportation was too inefficient to bring the throngs of visitors the success of the resort required. A new plan involved building a nine-mile, narrow-gauge railroad from the docks at Oak Bluffs to the outskirts of Edgartown and then onward to the development at Katama. Darrow and Bradley chose not to participate, but the other members of the Oak Bluffs Land and Wharf Company threw themselves enthusiastically into the new venture.

Carpenter, Collins and Norton each invested personal funds in the project and put up 17.5 percent of the total $40,000 cost. The largest investment by far, however, was that of the Town of Edgartown, which contributed

$15,000 that it borrowed from two off-island banks. This act of financial hubris resulted in condemnation by the *Vineyard Gazette*, even though its publisher, Edgar Marchant, was an incorporator. It seemed like a moneymaker; after all, railroads were booming. Thirty-three thousand miles of track—including the transcontinental line completed in 1869—had been laid from 1862 to 1873.

What could possibly go wrong?

The answer turned out to be "practically everything."

CHAPTER THREE

The Panic of 1873

The worst possible moment to build a new railroad had struck as work on the Martha's Vineyard Railroad began. When the line was completed in 1874, ticket sales were tepid and limited to the summer months. It's most persistent problem, however, was its tracks. The ties and rails were laid along the Oak Bluffs waterfront and along the low strip of sand that is now State Beach. Grafton Norton Collins's mariner's eye saw they would likely be swept away by wind, wave and tide and he argued for a more sheltered—but more expensive—route further inland. He wasn't heard. The railroad had to be partially rebuilt each spring to undo the damage done by winter storms.

Nearly $91,000 was ultimately spent on the Martha's Vineyard Railroad, which limped through twenty-two years of operations without ever turning a profit. It closed in 1896, leaving behind financial default and a right of way marked by raised roadbeds in the Katama woods, pilings and groins along Nantucket Sound still visible at low tide today.

The rail line was sold at auction for $16,250 in 1879 to cover unpaid taxes for the years 1876 and 1877.

Cottage City

A *Porter's American Monthly* correspondent, writing in 1877, reported that "Oak Bluffs exceeded our anticipation…the walks along its borders next to the ocean having no equal, within our knowledge, except that of the Cliffs at Newport. The cottages are numerous, large and attractive."

The leaders of Edgartown, whose town center was being eclipsed by the new summer resort, could not have been happy. The article mentioned Edgartown village only in the context of being connected to Oak Bluffs by its railroad.

Under tremendous financial stress, the partners of the Oak Bluffs Land and Wharf Company also had little reason to be happy. People continued to visit Oak Bluffs and build homes on lots they had purchased, but the company was obligated to provide repairs and render service to the new community it had brought into existence. Edgartown was unwilling to assist. The town had invested $15,000 into the railroad to take visitors away from Oak Bluffs and another $70,000 to build a road from Oak Bluffs to Edgartown in 1872. It refused, however, to construct a bridge over the opening to Lagoon Pond, which would have benefitted residents of Oak Bluffs by shortening the six-mile trip to Vineyard Haven. Taxes paid by the fifteen thousand seasonal homeowners in Oak Bluffs accounted for over 60 percent of Edgartown's revenues, but the five hundred year-round residents were refused fire or police protection.

It wasn't long before the cries for secession began to crescendo. The movement was backed by twenty-five prominent Oak Bluffs taxpayers and led by three year-round residents: Joseph Dias, a retired whaling captain who was the principal owner of the Vineyard Grove House hotel; boat builder Ichabod Norton Luce of Farm Neck, who was not only a vigorous secessionist but also a widely known abolitionist; and businessman Howes Norris of Eastville, whose business interests included a wharf on the east side of Vineyard Haven Harbor, near the present hospital. Norris used his money to buy the press and equipment of the struggling *Island Review* newspaper and used it to publish a new paper, the *Cottage City Star*, the first serious rival to the Edgartown-focused *Gazette*. The *Star* printed news from across the island (everywhere but Edgartown) and advocated tirelessly for secession.

Splitting off the northern part of Edgartown as its own town would require an act of the state legislature. That, in turn, required a change in representation. When calls for secession began, the Vineyard's representative to the state legislature was Beriah T. Hillman, who had become a leading citizen of Edgartown and was firmly aligned with its interests. Opposed by Edgartown, and so by Hillman, petitions for secession died on the floor of the legislature three years in a row. In the election of November 4, 1879, however, Hillman was narrowly defeated, 449 votes to 409, by Stephen Flanders of Chilmark. Flanders owed his plurality to two groups: "colored" residents of Oak Bluffs and Wampanoag men from Gay Head who had recently been granted the right to vote. Twenty-four of the twenty-five new voters from Gay Head cast their ballots for Flanders, and an attempt by Hillman supporters to throw out the entire Gay Head vote failed.

After the election, Hillman supporters composed—and circulated in Edgartown—an insulting parody of a popular children's song aimed at the group they blamed for their loss. Norris reprinted it in the *Star* under the headline "Stolen Thunder," describing it as "an attempt at parody at the expense of our worthy colored friends" and expressing the hope that "our Gay Head friends will read this 'poem.'"

> *One little nigger feeling rather blue,*
> *Sent for another nig to vote for Flanders too.*
> *Three little niggers thought they needed more*
> *Sent for another nig and that made four.*
> *Four little niggers feared their number small,*
> *Beckoned to another nig just within call.*
> *Six little niggers standing in the hall,*
> *Shouted for the seventh nig as loud as they could bawl.*
> *Seven little niggers knew their cause was great,*
> *Called for another nig, and that made eight.*
> *Eight little niggers standing in a line,*
> *Called for another nig, and that made nine.*
> *Nine little niggers—neither voting men,*
> *Called for another nig and that made ten.*
> *Up stepped Ichabod now to applaud,*
> *And praise the little nigs who helped in the fraud.*[50]

Flanders took his seat in the legislature and shepherded through legislation to split off the northern parts of Edgartown—Oak Bluffs, Wesleyan Grove, Vineyard Highlands and Eastville—as the new town of Cottage City. It became independent on February 17, 1880. Erastus Carpenter was delighted, Edgartown homeowner and stalwart Grafton Collins less so.

The End of the Oak Bluffs Land and Wharf Company

In 1878, the Oak Bluffs Land and Wharf Company sold the Sea View House hotel, along with the wharf, boardwalk and bathhouses, to Henry Brownell, whose company—Bullock and Brownell—had been the hotel's management team. The sale brought the company $110,000, which it used to pay down debts. The *Boston Herald*'s story on the sale summed up the problem: the company had "expended several hundred thousands of dollars in improvements, or considerably more than has ever been received from the sale of its lots."

Three years later, seeking ways to recoup more funds through the sale of land, the Oak Bluffs Land and Wharf Company floated a plan promoted by Erastus Carpenter to offer the town ownership of Ocean, Waban, Hartford and Pennacook Parks, along with nine avenues. The plan contradicted Carpenter's earlier assurances to buyers that the company had never actually conveyed the land or counted it among its assets. Grafton Norton Collins was inalterably opposed to the plan, insisting the company had no authority to make such a gift. Shubael Norton, who had mortgaged what was left of his farm in a last-ditch effort to keep the company afloat, agreed with Collins that the parks ought to be sold, strongly disagreeing with Carpenter.

It isn't patently clear if Carpenter's purpose was desperation, extortive or a practical means of pricing the parks for sale. Over a multiyear period, the town refused to decide what to do about the ostensible gift, so Carpenter changed tactics in 1884, offering to sell the parks to the town for $7,500 payable over twenty-five years, interest free. The town still refused to move. In March 1885, the company's investors lost patience and insisted that the parks be put up for sale, and the company admitted defeat; its business life had outlived its future. It proffered a sale to Boston attorney George C. Abbott and his partner Alvin Neal for $7,500, and a convoluted legal battle ensued. The OBLWC directors were split, at times agreeing the parks had value on the open market but at others agreeing that they should remain the property of the town. Ultimately, though, the OBLWC directors—except Collins, who sided with Abbott—testified that the parks could not be separately sold. The case went to trial in May 1886, and the judge ruled against the town, declaring that the parks were Abbott's property and that he was free to sell them if he wished. The town appealed to the Massachusetts Supreme Judicial Court in 1887, and in an opinion delivered by U.S. Supreme Court justice Oliver Wendell Holmes Jr., the court overturned the ruling.

Today, arriving on a ferry, Oak Bluffs, framed by Ocean Park, is the picture visitors see in their mind's eye when they think of Martha's Vineyard, the iconic scene created by the passion of the captains of Cottage City. Oak Bluffs' nine original parks—Ocean, Hartford, Waban, Penacook, Niantic, Hiawatha, Naushon, Nashawena and Petaluma—comprised twenty-five acres, fully a third of the new town's total area. Oak Bluffs—recognized as the town with the most parks per capita worldwide—continues to fulfill Erastus Carpenter's dream.

And the stories continued.

Charles Tallman

The hapless Charles Tallman of Osterville, missing his assignment on the bark *Bounding Billow*, instead joined the schooner *Christina* as first mate on a trip to Boston, sailing from Brooklyn on January 4, 1866, with Captain Leach and four others. Stopping overnight on January 5 at Holmes Hole (Vineyard Haven), where Tallman's brother in-law Reverend J.N. Collier was the Baptist minister, the *Christina* resumed its fateful trip the next day only to be caught in a blizzard-fueled nor'easter off Chappaquiddick's shallow Hawes Shoal. While stranded, probably aggravated by its cement cargo, and with a shattered keel, the ship's anchor swung loose and bashed opened the hull, causing it to sink on Sunday, January 7. That Monday, with gale winds and a frigid twenty-degree-below-zero temperature, a

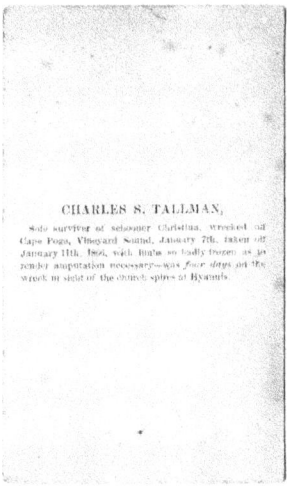

Charles S. Tallman. *Courtesy of the Martha's Vineyard Museum.*

woman spotted the ship's masts with Tallman and the crew clinging to the rigging in the wind and waves of the storm. With no reasonable way to save them during the storm, it took until Thursday, January 11, for a whaleboat manned by Captain Thomas Dunham and five others to rescue Charles Tallman. The sole survivor of the four days and nights of icy weather, his nightmare continued due to the frostbite that took most of his fingers and left his hands and legs mutilated. Cared for in Holmes Hole for weeks when part of his legs and feet were amputated, Tallman was called "one of nature's noblemen" by the *Vineyard Gazette*. Nicknamed "Shipwrecked Tallman," the ironic name for a literal wash-ashore who probably never again left land, he became a beloved character of the new town. To support himself, he sold peanuts and pictures of himself with notes on the back about his experience. Sometime between his rescue and 1874, the Oak Bluffs Land and Wharf Company built him an octagonal pavilion at the base of Ocean Park. Construction of his peanut stand began with tragedy but was consummated by the warmth of community. In the summer of 1877, he sold eighty-five bushels of peanuts.

Lover's Rock. *Courtesy of the Martha's Vineyard Museum.*

Bathing and Beaches

Promoted as a "Summer Residence by the Sea," sales literature extolled its virtues as "the healthiest and pleasantest watering-place of the country" with "the finest views of Vineyard Sound," "the soft and balmy atmosphere" and the "moderate temperature of the water attributable to the proximity of the Gulf Stream." Bathing was a new social activity, and swimming was unheard of until the 1890s. Bathing consisted of standing in the water chest-deep, fully clothed, and was an activity pursued largely by women and children. Women arrived in high-bustled dresses and used rented bathhouses to change into outfits almost as elaborate, replete with tights, with the only exposed body parts being faces and hands. Most people at the beach in those days were gawkers dressed in street clothes who mobbed the boardwalks and bathhouses to watch those who had adopted the new pastime of standing around in the water, specifically from 10:00 a.m. to 2:00 p.m. on sunny days, but not on Sundays. Photographs show few men in the water until the latter 1880s—similarly dressed head to toe—and it wasn't until the 1890s that

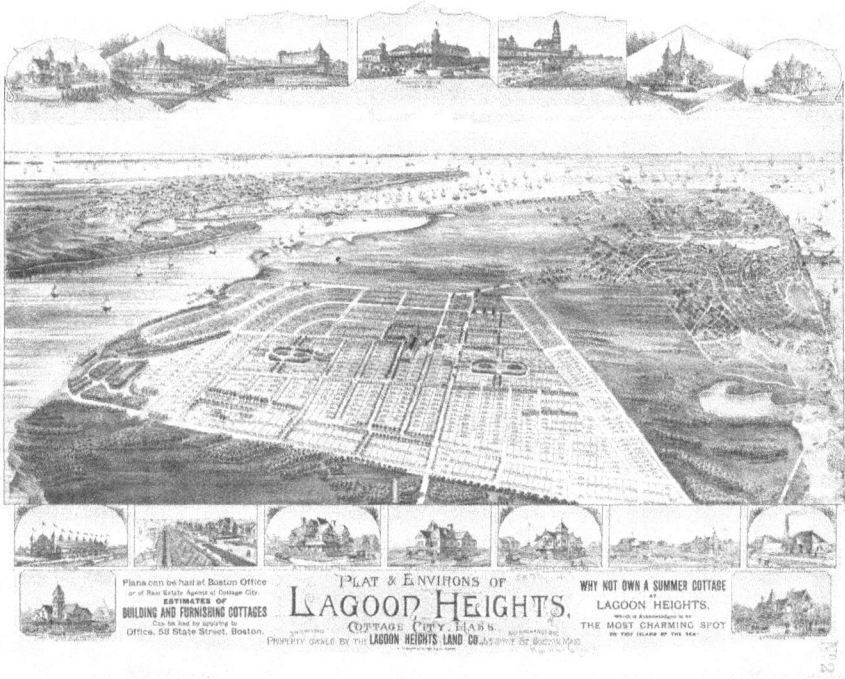

Plan of Lagoon Heights. *Courtesy of the Norman B. Leventhal Map & Education Center at the Boston Public Library.*

bathing suits became sleeveless. Bathing suits were made of a rough, heavy cotton material that held water and did not dry quickly, and one can only imagine how they must have smelled after a saltwater soak. A columnist for the *Boston Traveller* described a lady's suit:

> *It was composed of dark blue serge, pants of the same, trimmed with white. The sleeves came half-way between the shoulder and the elbow, and were scalloped and bound with white. The tunic, for that was the shape, reached just below the knee, also bound and scalloped, belt round, with white pink stockings and sandal slippers. A neat straw hat completed the costume.*

Articles and reviews about bathing suits were derisive to the point of insult. In 1886, the *Martha's Vineyard Herald* wrote, "The amount of physical beauty necessary to render a man sitting on the sand, clad in his bathing suit and nothing else, is possessed, possibly, by one in a thousand. Such an Adonis may be tolerated, with patience, but the nine hundred and ninety-nine unlovely dudes and nondescripts, should hide their ugliness beneath the waves."

Views of the water were completely blocked by rows of wooden bathhouses. John Walter, an editor of the *Dukes County Intelligencer*, described them as "the ugly, boxlike structures obliterating views of the water and occupying great swatches of sand."

These structures lined Oak Bluffs' Town and Highland Beaches until 1944, when the last one was removed.[51]

REAL ESTATE AND NEIGHBORHOOD DEVELOPMENTS

The speculation of Oak Bluffs knew no bounds. The entire town is about 4,500 acres. In 1873, there were 1,308 acres available for sale in Oak Bluffs: 400 in Ocean Heights and Englewood, 300 in Lagoon Heights and Grovedale, 225 in the Vineyard Highlands, 165 acres in Bellevue Heights, 120 in Oak Bluffs, 20 in Wesleyan Grove, 20 in Forest Hill, 15 in Oak Grove, 15 in Sea View Hill, 12 in Central Place, 10 in Sunset Heights and 6 in Bay View. Put another way, from 1866 to 1873, a seven-year period, 2,616 acres—close to 60 percent of the entire town—was on the market.

Hindsight, always the arbiter, illustrates why only that of the Land and Wharf Company met the test of time.

Lucy Vincent Smith

In January 1929, Lucy P. Vincent Smith was asked to write about the Cottage City of fifty years prior. The three-and-a-half-page document at the Martha's Vineyard Museum was typed from her handwriting, and notes on it indicate that she was born in 1842 and died in 1933, so she was eighty-seven when she wrote it. She had a great sense of humor. Acknowledging that Cottage City hadn't come into being in 1879, she wrote a brief introduction of how Captain Shubael L. Norton and his cohorts had begun the new Oak Bluffs development. We know the Campground community "became alarmed" and hurriedly built a tall fence to keep the new "noisy disturbing element" out. What I learned was that there were two gates, one at Pennacook Avenue and another at the end of Circuit Avenue. Lucy Smith recounted going "Bluffing" with several other young people in 1868 after services one night. She wrote, "The moon was just rising as we reached the Bluffs trailing through a narrow path cut through the woods."

This was before the boardwalks had been built and before Etta Godfrey's 1872 song "The Oak Bluffs Galop." Policemen were stationed at both gates to keep people out after curfew, and she and her friends had to run back so the fastest could beg for the gate to be kept open for the laggards. Lucy was apparently the fastest. They shared a tent in the Campgrounds divided in two, with girls on one side and the brother of one of the girls on the other. She told how buckets were to be kept filled with water at the back of tents in the event of fire. The water was from two pumps, one near the association building and the other at County Park. The gap and circumstance are unexplained, but she wrote about her whaling captain husband returning in 1869 from a trip of "three years and eight months." Though he planned to ship out again with his family, she decided they needed some time off alone, and "we boarded son in Edgartown then at a troublesome age, full of mischief realizing it would be no rest to take care of him at such a place as the Camp Ground then was and came not out of town for this was still a part of Edgartown generally called 'Eastville.'"

It's nice to know kids were the same in the 1860s as they are now—and interesting to find that even then parents with means knew what to do with them. The Smiths had an enjoyable vacation and bought a home before the next trip. Lucy and her husband found housing for their son and were able to take a short vacation in a room in the building that housed the Oak Bluffs Land and Wharf Company offices at the head of the new wharf.

Lucy wrote, "Lots were being sold, cottages were being built, everything booming. Stores, hotels being planned for. A lot for chapel had a few trees cut down and a sign marked 'Chapel Hill' placed on it." (This was to become Union Chapel.)

Her account of Oak Bluffs being built is the only first-person description I've discovered. It's clear that she and her husband loved the new town, and in a telling statement, Lucy wrote that if they "lived to return" from the voyage they'd like a summer home here.

In fact, she and her husband, Captain George A. Smith, sailed from New Bedford on the *Nautilus* to the Pacific on October 6, 1869, and returned on May 27, 1874. (The trip resulted in 154 barrels of sperm oil, 2,761 barrels of whale oil and 14,050 pounds of whale bone with a value of $93,470, worth approximately $2,067,000 in 2019.)

Lots with water views were all taken or too expensive, so they finally chose lot 178, which had a deed with a restriction that a house be built within two years. A carpenter friend from New Bedford built the home while they were on the whaling trip. When they returned after the four-year, eight-month voyage, they found "what a change! A city of cottages had sprung up. Hotels, stores, concrete streets where only sand had been….The Lot we bought that summer almost out in the woods, cleared and built on, and surrounded by other houses."

Lucy was surprised that the small clearing in the woods where services were held at the Sacred Tree on the last Sunday of camp meetings had become Hartford Park between Pequot and Massasoit Avenues. The grand Sea View House hotel had been built, along with a skating rink near the old rooming house they had stayed in—which had been taken down and rebuilt as the Island House hotel. "Circuit Avenue was filled with stores, hotels and a few drinking houses, past Pennacook Avenue."

As the years wore on, Lucy described "murmerings of dissatisfaction were heard saying that heavy taxes were being paid to Edgartown and little returns received in improvements, that more money was being used in Edgartown, than here." She retold the story of events that led to the secession and Edgartown's Oak Bluffs neighborhood becoming the new independent town of Cottage City. Her letter is a first-person account of the times as a witness to the building of the fabulous town we enjoy today. Poignantly, she wrote: "it has come and gone, lasting only 27 years from 1880–1907 when it became Oak Bluffs." Her letter ends, "May peace and prosperity abide, within its borders. May the coming 49 years be as prosperous as the past 49 have been."

William Claflin Cottage. Substantially altered, the cottage is at the corner of Pequot and Sea View Avenues. *Courtesy of the Martha's Vineyard Museum.*

Lucy would have loved how things turned out. Lucy P. Vincent Smith and her husband George A. Smith's lot 178 is the house at 79 Circuit Avenue, on the corner of the Bayliss Avenue entrance to the Campground, now occupied by the Good Dog Goods store.

Iconic Architects and Architecture

Oak Bluffs has a fairly unique architectural history. After 1835, when Wesleyan Grove was established for the Campground, frequent annual visitors staked out plots encircling the preacher's stand that were sold to them by the Martha's Vineyard Camp Meeting Association. Families erected tents to house themselves during their often summer-long stay and devised intricate ropes tied atop them to differentiate one from another. Over time and to reflect permanence, the tenting became wood and resulted in the Victorian "gingerbread" homes worldwide travelers come to see today. This type of design and construction, portraying its social and religious mores, lent itself to what has been called America's only original architecture, "Camp Ground" or "Carpenter" Gothic Revival, by Ellen Weiss.[52]

Ellen Weiss

Ellen Weiss, a now-retired professor from the Tulane School of Architecture, is a writer and Vineyarder who, along with her book *City in the Woods*, about the Campground, is the author of *Robert R. Taylor and Tuskegee: An African American Architect Designs for Booker T. Washington*. Taylor (June 8, 1868–December 13, 1942) was the son of a freed slave (Henry Taylor), himself the son of a white slave owner and a black mother.[53]

Robert Taylor

Robert Taylor was the first African American student to attend the Massachusetts Institute of Technology in 1888 and graduated with his degree in architecture in 1892. Robert Taylor considered his design of Tuskegee College (an HBCU) the best of his career. Evidenced by his correspondence with Booker T. Washington from here in Cottage City, he also had island ties.[54]

His great-granddaughter Valerie Jarrett, an advisor to former president Barack Obama, has a home in Oak Bluffs.[55] There is a U.S. Postal Service stamp with his picture, and the stamp is on an envelope Joe Vera sent me postmarked June 4, 2015.[56]

Robert Taylor postage stamp. *Courtesy of the U.S. Postal Service.*

In the Campground, Perez Mason, an architect from Providence, was employed by many to design the wooden cottages that were to replace the semi-permanent tents, beginning with the association's office building in 1859. Mason also designed the wood-covered preacher's stand centered in the circle of homes in 1861.

As the summer religious community grew—upwards of 12,000 attended Camp Meeting Week in 1865—it also outgrew the small preacher's stand, so in 1879, J.W. Hoyt, a Campgrounder and engineer from Springfield, Massachusetts, designed the iron tabernacle in use today for $7,147.84.[57]

Samuel Freeman Pratt (1824–1920)

The man who had the most architectural impact on the new development was Samuel Freeman Pratt. In addition to many of the commercial structures of Oak Bluffs, Pratt designed between eighteen and twenty-two homes, about twelve of which remain.[58]

Some are easily spotted on Canonicus and Samoset Avenues. Several are on Narragansett, Pequot and Tuckernuck Avenues, and each is a carved wooden work of art. We know little about his early life (his father was a carpenter), but his midlife was spent as an architect, and he designed some of Martha's Vineyard's most engaging structures between 1870 and 1872. Pratt designed the gateway to the wharf in Oak Bluffs, the first and most majestic Sea View House Hotel, the Arcade on Circuit Avenue, a band pavilion on Seaview Avenue (long gone) and Union Chapel. He had no known architectural training, and other than these mentioned, he designed just two hotels at Katama and on New York's Shelter Island and his own home in Newport. That was the whole of his architectural career. He became wealthy from a sewing machine patent and lived the rest of his life in Newport as a gentleman of leisure. The sample homes for sale on Robert Morris Copeland's maps were Pratt's designs. His work is characterized as having a dynamic and festive style similar to sixteenth-century French secular buildings. Ellen Weiss described his designs as having "activated skylines with jerkinhead gables, candlesnuffers, steep-hipped roofs, finials, dormers, and eaves that kick out, bending roof and dormer lines at their edges in a lilting fashion."

Pratt specialized in mansard roofs, where the second- or third-floor roof lines are less sharp than those at the top, in an effort to increase interior room size and affect a taller look for otherwise small homes. Typically, the mansard roof is used to add majesty to homes, at times making room for a third floor. Over the years, most of the remaining homes were severely modified, and many are difficult to recognize. An easy-to-spot Pratt home is at 16 Narragansett Avenue. It was originally the Blood Cottage, built for railroad magnate Hiram Blood, who coined the phrase "The Cottage City of America."

Samuel Freeman Pratt's brilliant designs and America's only original architecture throughout the Campgrounds made Oak Bluffs famous worldwide.

THE PINK HOUSE

The iconic Pink House is among the most photographed and most deservedly remains a postcard.[59] Ellen Weiss would describe this heirloom as a wood-frame home with tongue-and-groove vertical boarding, a Campground cottage of cross-gable Gothic design with decorative pediment and balustrades and post-and-bracket construction. We just call it the Pink House—and everyone knows which it is despite there actually being nine houses of varying degrees of pinkness. On the corner of Butler Avenue and Jordan Crossing, the house has pink siding, deeper pink trim and pink throughout the inside. It wasn't always pink. Built between 1864 and 1868, it was one of the earlier Campground homes. Pink may have been frivolous in the early religious Campground days if not scandalous, like writer Mary Jane Carpenter's story in the *Vineyard Gazette* explains:

> *The first owner, whose name is unknown to me, was the one who embellished it with many types of fancy jigsaw trimmings, which don't match each other. There are two very old stories told about this trim. One is that the first owner had an affair with the carpenter who did all the trim work around the Camp Ground and he gave her the trim cuttings. The other is that the woman got all the trim at the dump and attached it to her house.*

Past owners were Lillian Cotton Impey (1940s), Jean VanVliet Spencer (1950s, who first painted the house pink) and Anita and Jack Welles. The Welleses, who painted the house the deep pink color it remains, signed the offering letter for the cottage appropriately enough on Valentine's Day. The next owner was from Falmouth and delighted in coming over on the ferry

The Pink House. *Courtesy of the* Vineyard Gazette.

to her pink cottage. Sold most recently in 2014, the Pink House looks as if it could have been Hansel and Gretel's gingerbread cottage.

The folks at the Campground, calling the new community of the Oak Bluffs Land and Wharf Company "ungodly," demonstrated their disdain in 1867 by erecting the seven-foot picket fence around the Campground Lucy P. Vincent Smith wrote of. To address the issue—and since there was nowhere for the new community of visitors to worship—the Oak Bluffs Land and Wharf Company had Samuel Pratt design Union Chapel as a nonsectarian place of worship that cost $16,000 to build. With a unique octagonal shape, it was completed in a year, seating eight hundred with a ninety-six-foot spire. Some meetings that led to secession were held in Union Chapel, and it hosted town meetings and high school graduations for a number of years. Its once-proud tower was lost in a storm, and many long for a time when its owner, the Vineyard Trust, might consider renovating it to its original glory. Built on the small mound of Chapel Hill, the architecturally significant church opened in August 1871 and was listed in the National Register of Historic Places in 1990.

Little did the participants of Cottage City know how much influence the Panic of 1873 would have on the Oak Bluffs Land and Wharf Company's new resort.

Tarleton Cadwallader Luce

Tarleton C. Luce. *Courtesy of the Martha's Vineyard Museum.*

It's unknown how Ichabod Norton Luce's cousin Tarleton Cadwallader Luce gained his fortune, but his sale of part of the Vineyard Highlands to the Vineyard Grove Company in 1869 certainly added to it. He acquired a substantial portion of Eastville—where Ichabod and his neighbor Ebenezer Lamson owned two of the few homes—from former whale captain Shubael Hawes Norton. By the time Ichabod and Tarleton joined the new Dukes County Savings Bank in 1872, Tarleton Luce had struck out on his own to develop Bellevue Heights, a 921-plot parcel of land that bordered (and extended beyond) Eastville Avenue, Towanticut Avenue, and about half of the Highlands around Crystal Lake and along Temahigan Avenue. The appealing map and plan dated June 22, 1872, no doubt helped sales; nine lots were sold for $2,000 in a single week, and Luce and others continued the buying and selling spree with ever more growing returns.

The spree didn't last.

The ebullience of the ad in the *Vineyard Gazette* of September 5, 1873, missed no opportunity for hyperbole in describing the opportunity of ownership in the new Bellevue Heights development at Eastville. Running for three months, the ad described the gently undulating slope towards the water, the fine views of the shipping passage of Vineyard Sound and the exceedingly healthy air, tempered by the sea breeze, which is always cool and healthy. A part I particularly enjoyed was the comparative notion of the "entire freedom from conventionalities of the more pretentious watering places," an apt description even today. Replete with a poem— "There is a pleasure in the pathless woods / There is a rapture on the lonely shore / There is society where none intrude, by the deep sea, and music in its roar"—the advertisement entreated buyers and extolled the high moral character of its residents. On reflection, constructing homes on the 921 tastefully laid out small lots, measuring fifty by one hundred feet, would have decimated the woods, pathless or not.

Bellevue Heights was one of eighteen Oak Bluffs subdivisions being advertised in 1873. Developer Tarleton Cadwallader Luce had ambitiously planned to build an opera house on the property. Placing the magnitude of Luce's plan in perspective, the Oak Bluffs Land and Wharf Company paid $1,242 in taxes compared with Luce's $522. Luce, born in Edgartown in 1822, married Martha Daggett Luce in 1854, and they had a son, William Cristant Luce, who was born in 1864. America's economic malaise of 1873 was nothing but bad news for "T.C." Luce, as he called himself.

Unnoticed by island developers, investors and lenders, from 1866 to 1873, America had built thirty-five thousand miles of railroad track. This construction was largely provided for by the banking firm of Jay Cooke and Company, the chief financier of the Union army in the Civil War. On September 18, 1873, recognizing it was overextended, the Cooke Company declared bankruptcy. This precipitated the Panic of 1873, when many other banks and industries did the same. Close to 90 of the nation's 364 railroads collapsed, 18,000 businesses failed, and by 1876, unemployment had risen to 14 percent.

This didn't contribute to a demand for second homes, and Luce, absent buyers and losing $60,000, filed for bankruptcy in February 1874. Sometime after the failure of Bellevue Heights, Luce was spirited away from Oak Bluffs one night either from embarrassment or, more likely, to avoid payment of his obligations to debtors, one of whom was surely Shubael H. Norton, from whom he acquired the land. Captain Norton took the former Luce house and had it moved to a new location where it is today, at 29 Laurel Avenue in the Highlands.[60]

There is substantial evidence that Tarleton Cadwallader Luce removed himself to the small town of White Rock, California, about twenty miles northeast of Sacramento. There he, his wife and son lived with his mother, Prudence. He is said to have taken up carpentry as an occupation and was apparently divorced from Martha before his death, sometime between 1882 and 1892.[61]

Ironically, over time, the developers were proven correct; after their losing substantial sums of money, Oak Bluffs survived to become the summer resort we know today.

CHAPTER FOUR

THE GREAT HOTELS: 1871–79

The first structure built at the wharf by the Oak Bluffs Land and Wharf Company was originally a storehouse with office space used by Samuel Lyman Norton. It had rooms upstairs that Captain and Lucy Smith stayed in. It was later repurposed to become the Island House Hotel and was moved to Circuit Avenue (today it has rooms above a restaurant and bar establishment but is no longer a hotel). This is where the historic Sea View House hotel was constructed, and many believe, due to its size and opulence, that it was Oak Bluffs' first general hotel.

Highland House Hotel

In fact, the Highland House hotel first opened on June 1, 1871. The Vineyard Grove Company was established in 1868 to protect the Campgrounds from the secular activities of the new part of town. It was this company that built the Highland House, which was expected to compete with the Oak Bluffs Land and Wharf Company in the event the Campground would have to be moved farther away from the less-than-religious new Cottage City development. The Campground Association itself refused investing in the plan, so backed by shares sold to members of the Methodist community, the Vineyard Grove Company acquired 300 acres of today's Highlands neighborhood for its own development. It built its own wharf at the base of East Chop, so ferries had to make two stops in Oak Bluffs very near to each other. Vineyard Grove built the majestic four-story, mansard-roofed Highland House hotel at what is now the East Chop Beach Clubhouse. The company also built a 3,500-foot boardwalk that extended from the hotel across the then-closed Lake Anthony (which had been called Squash Meadow Pond) and over to the North Bluff. Guests used the boardwalk for access to the beachfront with two hundred bathhouses. The Highlands development, like others—Bellevue Heights, Oakland, Prospect Heights, Central Place, Forest Hill, Oak Grove and Lagoon Heights—missed the anticipated wave of prosperity, and by 1880, all of these areas were incorporated, post secession, into the town of Cottage City. The Highland House was principally owned by John D. Flint, Clofus L. Gonyon and Augustus G. Wesley (who would later become owner and manager of the Wesley House). It was burned down in the fall of 1893, apparently by an arsonist who plundered the empty hotel before the fire.

Sea View House

Completed in 1872 for $132,000, the opulent, Samuel F. Pratt–designed Sea View House hotel was 300 feet long and five stories tall, with 125 rooms and a dining hall that could seat 400. Constructed at the head of the Oak Bluffs Land and Wharf Company's ferry terminal on the water, the new hotel rapidly captured the imagination and hyperbole of travel writers and embodied the new seaside watering place.

On May 3, 1885, the *New York Times* published;

> *The Sea View House and land with wharf adjoining, octagonal restaurant, 280 bathing houses, the land on which the skating rink and carousel are standing, and the entire shore of Oak Bluffs, comprising the strip of land east of Sea View Avenue…was acquired at auction by the Vineyard Grove Company for $32,000, a fraction of the 1866 investment of $300,000.*

It was certainly fitting that the owners of the Vineyard Grove Company, members of the Campground Methodist community, would wind up owning the balance of the new resort town their efforts had contributed to building. In 1895, the Vineyard Grove Company sought to build a pavilion over Town Beach, a move vigorously opposed by the adjoining homeowners. Out of character for the Campground but well within the limits of Cottage City,

Sea View House hotel. *Courtesy of the Martha's Vineyard Museum.*

the move led to a lawsuit from nearby homeowners who believed the 1885 sale included covenants preventing buildings that would block views and the beach. In a decision favoring the homeowners, Supreme Court justice Oliver Wendell Holmes found that the open space was dedicated to the public with the view of the sea from the bluff a valid part of the argument. Peace prevailed, but the issue resurfaced again after Lake Anthony was opened to the sea (in 1900), destroying the 3,500-foot wooden boardwalk, and the land was sold for cottages built along the shore. That time the company prevailed, and today, those are the homes and buildings behind Our Market along East Chop Drive.

At 11.45 on Saturday night, watchman Lewis rung in the alarm from box 41, at the Arcade, and people jumped from their beds and rushes to the windows and saw, with dismay, the eastern sky brilliantly illuminated, directly over the Sea View House. Cries of "Fire!" "Fire!" "The Sea View House!" "The Sea View House!!" rent the stillness of the night, the light in the heavens contrasting vividly with the darkness, the sky being overcast with heavy clouds, from which at times the rain descended, as if weeping in sorrow over the awful catastrophe.[62]

Its legend outlasted its short twenty-year life. The Sea View House was one of several that burned down over the years, with others torn down for their lumber when a fractured American economy didn't need as many rooms. There were almost twenty original hotels built, some more renowned than others, like the Central House (the renamed Dunbar House), where President Grant dined in 1874, and the Vineyard Grove House, where some secession meetings were held.[63]

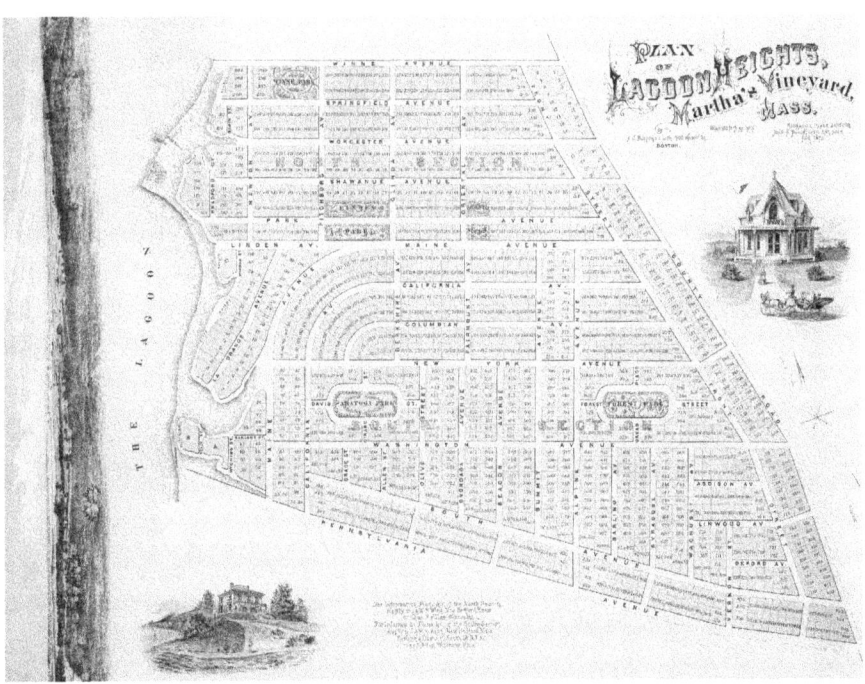

Plan of Lagoon Heights. *Courtesy of the Norman B. Leventhal Map & Education Center at the Boston Public Library.*

Prospect House

Less remains of Prospect House than many of the other fabulous Cottage City hotels. Impresario Erastus Carpenter's halo was glowing, and other developers thought to strike while the iron was hot. The Lagoon Heights development was mapped out in 1873 for the sale of five hundred lots in the area bordered by County Road and Pennsylvania Avenue. The highly ornamental three-and-a-half story, mansard-roofed Prospect House hotel was built on a one-hundred-by-one-hundred-foot plot at the corner of Hudson and Beacon Avenues (a dirt road today) for prospective buyers to stay at while considering their investment. Its principal feature, besides accommodations for two hundred guests, was views across the Lagoon to Vineyard Haven and to downtown Oak Bluffs, as in those days the landscape, raised higher than the surrounding area, was barren of vegetation.

A trolley line was laid from downtown along Wing Road, left onto Alpine Avenue, then right onto Hudson with a stop at Prospect House that ended at the foot of Hudson Avenue on the Lagoon. The hotel received an addition and renovation in 1894, but alas, missing the building and economic boom, Lagoon Heights never quite caught on, and Prospect House burned to the ground in June 1898. Today, the park-like site is vacant of all but memories. Real estate super salesman Eben Davis Bodfish sold many of the lots, one of which was owned by his wife, Elizabeth. Neighbors shared the story of another hotel nearby, Reid's Hotel. It was on the southwest corner of Newton and Worcester Avenues and owned by Alexander Reid and his wife (at the time a widow) when the hotel caught fire and burned to the ground in 1937. Lacking fire hydrants, the firemen planned to use a pumper to siphon water from the Lagoon below to fight the fire but couldn't get it down to the beach.[64]

An apocryphal legend is that Oak Bluffs had once had a brothel, and the Reid may have been it.

The Wesley House

In a town filled with irony, colorful characters and stories, the Wesley House hotel stands alone. The harbor-front Victorian structure was built for $18,000 in 1879 by French Canadian cook Augusten Goupee, who changed his name to Augustus G. Wesley as a paean to John Wesley, the founder of Methodism. The Martha's Vineyard Campground Meeting Association still owns the land the hotel sits on. The hotel's story was told by its owner:

I, Augustus G. Wesley, of Cottage City, in the Commonwealth of Massachusetts, hereby make the following voluntary statement, of my own free will and accord, without hope or expectation of favor by reason of so doing, viz: Nov. 13, 1894, Tuesday evening, I went, from prayer meeting at the Methodist church in Cottage City to the Wesley hotel owned by me. I entered the hotel about half-past eight. I saturated some burlap in the closet under the stairs on the second floor with kerosene and wrapped it around a cigar box, in which I placed a lighted candle. I did this for the purpose of setting fire to the building and contents in order to collect the insurance on them.

Convicted on September 26, 1895, Wesley was sentenced to three years in the "house of correction" but was pardoned, not filing a claim, on July 29, 1897, "upon the recommendation of nearly all of Cottage City's prominent citizens and taxpayers."[65]

The ninety-five-room Wesley House was acquired, renovated and had its name changed to Summercamp by new owners in 2016. It is the sole remaining of the majestic Cottage City hotels, operating continuously as a hotel since it was built.[66]

1874

None of Oak Bluffs' years were as important to the town's future or popularity as 1874. By all accounts, that summer was the biggest and most exciting. Historian Arthur Railton wrote, "It was a watershed summer. There would be no turning back. The nation, in 1874, discovered our Island."[67]

Indeed, developers had over two thousand acres for sale, divided into neat rectangles of eight per acre, and speculation was rampant. Seventeen new hotels were in virtual walking distance and available to host madding crowds who had come to pray in the campground meetings or play on their outskirts. Vice President Henry Wilson stopped for a day, and the Hartford professional baseball team came for an exhibition game. A New York woman had $1,000 in jewelry stolen from her room at the Highland House. The national press had a field day after Samuel K. Elliott shot to death the brother of one of the two sisters who had chosen to live at Elliott's Tuckernuck Avenue home. These activities were eclipsed when President Ulysses S. Grant—the general who won the War Between the States—and a party of three hundred VIPs descended for a three-day stay.

Illumination and Fireworks

In 1869, Erastus Carpenter developed a real estate promotion, Illumination, as a sales aid to show off the new town on what he called Governor's Day for honoree Governor William Claflin, who owned one of the Pratt cottages facing the water on Seaview Avenue.[68] To draw attention to them, the few already-built homes would hang Japanese lanterns on porches.[69]

Initially, the Methodists in the Campground felt the displays to be ungodly—an opinion that changed over the years, which allowed for the promotion to be held in the Campground itself, a far more intimate venue, in honor of the visit of President Ulysses S. Grant on Friday, August 28, 1874. Illumination has continued since then when, at dark, one secret cottage has the honor of lighting the first lantern for all to follow. It remains a charming feature today, admired by as many as three thousand onlookers. Fireworks were also featured on two evenings of the president's historic visit, another tradition that continues. For over forty years in succession, the volunteer Oak Bluffs Fire Department has hosted a late-August fireworks display in Ocean Park. For countless families, the tradition is replete with deep memories of the fragrance of freshly cut grass decorated by beach blankets and spreads of all colors and, at dusk, the nighttime excitement of barely restrained children—and if you're lucky, my wife's fried chicken and macaroni salad and perhaps a slice or two of Giordano's Pizza. Add a few generations of family and friends, and the fireworks themselves are the punctuation of another great summer, the dessert of an enchanted evening.

Presidential Visit

In 1874, the president's visit popularized Oak Bluffs and made for national headlines as newspapers described every event, activity, church service and meal Ulysses S. Grant had on his trip. President Grant slept at Bishop Gilbert Haven's cottage in the Campground for three nights but spent little quality time on the Vineyard and, indeed, showed little interest in it or its people. He day tripped to Hyannis, Naushon and Nantucket while here. It was said Grant had come to Oak Bluffs for political reasons as he was contemplating running for a third term. A comment attributed to him was that "there were three political parties in America; Republicans, Democrats and Methodists"—and there were Methodists aplenty in Oak Bluffs. One evening, the president and his entourage were paraded around Oak Bluffs to experience Illumination a second time. Led by a brass band, the president and his party arrived at the Tucker cottage on Ocean Park, where they watched a spectacular fireworks display with thirty thousand others. There were no pictures of Grant smiling during his trip, and the *Gazette*'s Henry Beetle Hough noted the few words he spoke: "I thank you for your cheering greeting. No doubt you are tired and sleepy, as I am, so I will not detain you. Good Night."

Grant's wife, Julia, said she was "delighted with this island," the president made his usual bow, and they departed, but thanks to Grant's stay, Cottage City—Oak Bluffs—became the town people think of when they say Martha's Vineyard.

> *It is probable that the great majority of people who make reference by voice or pen to Martha's Vineyard are thinking when they do so, only of Cottage City, that place being the, grand centre of attractions and interests for the whole Island, and, indeed, the summering centre, par excellence, of all the land and water thereabouts.*[70]

The other eight leaders of the free world to visit the Vineyard (John Adams, Chester Arthur, William Clinton, Calvin Coolidge, Franklin D. Roosevelt, John F. Kennedy, Richard Nixon and Barack Obama) were at least a tad more verbose, excepting perhaps Franklin D. Roosevelt, who stayed aboard a sailboat during his trip. A 2016 ABC-TV Facebook page included a story wherein local shopkeeper and former selectman Todd Rebello, speaking about President Obama's visit, shared his view that in addition to the boost in our economy, if you're from Oak Bluffs, "No matter what your politics are, when the President of the United States chooses your community it's an absolute honor."

There were different kinds of fireworks in that all-important year too.

Killing and Murder in the News

While it is certain that there are more authors of murder mysteries on Martha's Vineyard than there have been actual murders, 1874 proved an exception. That year, sewing machine salesman Samuel K. Elliott of 89 Tuckernuck Avenue hired Mrs. P.R. Dexter as his housekeeper. She moved into the house along with her married sister, Lizzie C. Dickson, whose husband, Allen F. Dickson, was a sailor aboard a coastal schooner. The deputy sheriff of Dukes County, John N. Vinson, also lived in the house.

When Allen Dickson returned ashore in midsummer, he demanded his wife accompany him home, and she refused, wanting to stay with her sister until her child was born (there is no information in the story as to when the child may have been conceived). Outraged, Dickson gathered at the house the night of August 1 with four friends—one of whom, Caleb Smith, was the brother of the two ladies—with the intention of tarring and feathering Elliott. One of the armed vigilantes attempted to get Elliott out of the house. Elliott got his gun and wound up shooting Caleb Smith. After the fury of getting Elliott into a carriage to take him to the tarring and feathering spot, the group realized Smith had fallen out. They returned to recover him and rush him to the doctor, but it was too late. In the confusion, Elliott escaped and turned himself in for protection. Deputy Sherriff Vinson, fearing for his life, left the island, never to return. Massive press coverage followed the murder trial in the *Vineyard Gazette* and Boston and New York newspapers. Elliott's trial concluded with a verdict of self-defense. That September, the four remaining vigilantes were arraigned for aggravated assault and riotous conduct, but the grand jury was unable to indict, and the men were set free. The *Gazette* published a letter by Samuel Elliott, who proclaimed his innocence.

> *As regards any illegal proceedings at my house, there have been none....I hold myself in readiness to answer to the law at all times. What I have done, I am truly sorry for....It was wholly self-defense. If a party wishes to dictate who I shall have for a housekeeper, or who shall have board with me, I wish to know where they get their authority.*

The *Gazette* does not say what happened to the deputy sheriff, who was replaced by John Adams Pease, or the two women involved. Elliott left the island immediately.

Years later, the rape and murder of seventy-two-year-old Clara Smith on June 29, 1940, at the Phidelah Rice School of the Spoken Word on Arlington Avenue in East Chop was not only recorded but lauded as the first media circus on Martha's Vineyard. The sensational trial of the hapless Ralph Huntingdon Rice, a mild-mannered diction teacher and son of the institution's founder accused of the evildoing, was well covered by the eastern press until October 9, 1940, when he was acquitted of all charges. Harold Tracy, an electrician who had used the alias "Jan Thomas" and who lived and worked at the school, was finally indicted for the crime in 1942. On May 3, 1946, his hearing in Edgartown was dropped for lack of evidence, and the murder remains unsolved.

Agassiz Hall: The Martha's Vineyard Summer Institute

Agassiz Hall was the name of the building that housed the Martha's Vineyard Summer Institute, the fabled school for teachers that ironically overlooked Highland Beach, once used by black vacationers until it was taken over by the East Chop Beach Club. Its namesake was Louis Agassiz, a Swiss American biologist who founded a summer school on the Elizabethan Island of Pekinese, given to him in 1873 by John Anderson, a philanthropist who admired Agassiz's extensive work and contributions to science. Agassiz held several degrees and was an innovative scholar of zoology, geology and related areas. Although his work was widely acknowledged and respected, it was said that his revulsion on encountering African Americans in the United States caused him to spend much of his career rejecting Darwin's theory of evolution and attempting to prove that human races were of different origins (polygenism). This is contrary to the widely accepted concept of monogenism, the single origin of humanity. The Anderson school collapsed soon after Agassiz's death but is considered a model for the Woods Hole Institute and the Martha's Vineyard Summer Institute, established in Oak Bluffs in 1878 by Colonel Homer B. Sprague. With a modest start and few students, the institute began its career without funds or buildings, instead meeting "in cottage parlors and on piazzas, over offices and in tents." Martha's Vineyard was chosen due to its favorable conditions—"cool, quiet and health-giving…a summer watering-place, where the breezes, from whatever quarter they blow, are cooled and purified by the surrounding ocean, overlooking Vineyard Sound, the great marine highway between New York and Boston."[71] The business model was equally modest; each department head contributed to the expense and was paid by the tuition fees from his (or her) own pupils. Public lectures of interest to the folks of Cottage City were given in halls and churches, and the school ingratiated itself in a way to receive wide support. After four years, the Vineyard Grove Company gave the school a lot, and subscribers contributed enough money for a building with sixteen class rooms that was completed in 1882. In pioneering other such summer schools to follow, it was said that thousands of students who attended over the years came from "every state and territory in the union, as well as representatives from Canada, Mexico, South America, the Hawaiian Islands, and even England."[72] Instruction was given in esoteric courses like botany, didactics (the science of teaching), drawing, elocution (controlled speaking), English literature, entomology (the study of insects),

The Martha's Vineyard Summer Institute. *Courtesy of the Martha's Vineyard Museum.*

French, geology, German, Greek, Latin, mineralogy, pedagogy (the method and practice of teaching), philosophy, physical culture, phonography (a writing system representing sounds by individual symbols), vocal music and zoology each July through August until it closed in 1907. The institute described itself as "an educational institution whose beneficial influence has already been felt in every State of the Union; an institution that knows, in dispensing its benefits, no distinction of creed, race, or color."

So it was unsurprising to see in a photograph from the *Vineyard Gazette*'s archives taken in 1904 of sixty-seven people—forty-seven women, nineteen men and one toddler—that one of the women was black.

Agassiz wasted quite a bit of his time on a foolish thought.

COTTAGE CITY STAR

In May 1879, a group calling itself the Vineyard Publishing Association started the *Cottage City Star* in Vineyard Grove. The *Star*, a weekly newspaper (biweekly in July and August), was expressly founded to spearhead Oak Bluffs' effort to secede from Edgartown. The whaling industry was no longer able to support its economy, and Edgartown sought to both increase taxes and reduce or deny services for schools and safety. It refused to help fund the construction of the bridge to Vineyard Haven to prevent Oak Bluffs consumers from easily shopping up-island—even though taxation without representation had failed one hundred years earlier. The *Cottage City Star* portrayed Oak Bluffs in a more favorable light for the other island towns that would ultimately get to vote on the secession. Editor Howes Norris indicated that the movement was launched so the "oppressed section of Edgartown might give voice to their sentiments and have an aid in securing what they deemed their rights."

Notably, Howes was the namesake of his father, the notorious Captain Howes Norris of the whale ship *Sharon*. Captain Norris was murdered in a mutiny caused by his crazed killing of George Babcock, a mulatto steward, in 1842. In 1851, Norris's mother died when she was struck by lightning.[73]

CHAPTER FIVE

Freedom

An 1877 travel guide waxed eloquently,

> *As to Oak Bluffs, with its great number of first-class hotels, its countless cottages, beautiful as the abodes of fairy land, its excellent society, moral, intelligent, and high toned, yet reasonably open, democratic, and kindly disposed to all, the best and safest shore for bathing almost on the Atlantic coast—it is the most beautiful of the seaside resorts of Massachusetts.*[74]

In February 1879, before our incorporation as Cottage City in 1880, there were 769 cottages, 1,058 taxable buildings and 672 persons. There were also 2 steam mills, 17 major hotels, 2 markets, 2 blacksmiths, 7 grocery stores and 3 churches. Farm Neck, Eastville, Wesleyan Grove and of course the brand-new Oak Bluffs had consolidated into a township that continued to amaze visitors. With "themes of astonishment," we were transported into a "fairyland, a miniature city dedicated to joy, pervasive religious feeling, nature, and social density with our blatantly commercial edge."[75]

By our emancipation in 1907, Cottage City had become a misnomer due to the growth of the year-round population, and we reverted to Oak Bluffs.

Secession: 1880

In just over forty years, an entire town with over a thousand homes in over eighteen subdivisions had been built from a damp thicket of trees at the northeastern end of the island, but it was managed by the southernmost established town of Edgartown. The irony of such rampant growth ultimately causing contention probably couldn't have been predicted. The new community wound up paying the majority of the taxes but received slow and second-class service, since the majority of taxpayers were not voters but seasonal visitors. The costs of growth in Cottage City included police and fire, clean water and sewage, road construction and maintenance, health and schools—all signs of a town, from Edgartown's perspective, getting too big for its britches.

Largely responsible for Edgartown's growth, the unfortunate timing of the end of the whaling industry contributed to growing ill will, and almost one hundred years after the Revolution, the phrase "taxation without representation" was being heard from this new area off-islanders were freely referring to when they mentioned Martha's Vineyard. The seeds of secession were sown.

The new village's property value accounted for 60 percent of the taxes paid to Edgartown. With only five hundred year-round voting citizens, most taxes were paid by visitors who owned the majority of the seasonal property—a collection of buildings that was empty during winter. Essentially all political control rested in Edgartown, which profited from the new taxable property but gave little or nothing in return. For example, an Edgartown leader refused to fund a bridge to Vineyard Haven, cutting the new community off from easy access to the westernmost island towns. Conversely, when Edgartown decided to invest in building the Beach Road to tap into the new commerce, it was Cottage City taxpayers who objected. When the new citizenry realized that Edgartown had fallen into decline while the economy shifted to their new community, the salt of secession streamed through the otherwise sweet air. Secession was assured by the 1879 island-wide election of Chilmark's Stephen Flanders, a supporter of Cottage City's separation. That year's election was the first time Gay Head's original people were allowed to vote, and they, along with Farm Neck's black residents, helped pass the petition after three earlier attempts. At 4:40 p.m. on February 17, 1880, Governor Thomas Talbot signed the petition in the state legislature proclaiming Cottage City independent of Edgartown. The naming of the new town became one of many controversies. Residents wanted it named after their own neighborhoods, Vineyard Grove was preferred by the Camp Meeting Association, and Oak Bluffs was preferred by Oak Bluffs Land and Wharf neighbors. Finally, Hiram A. Blood (former mayor of Fitchburg, summer resident and owner of the Blood Cottage on Narragansett Avenue) suggested the compromise Cottage City. The new government devoted itself to the needs of the year-round community. With schools, fire and police departments, a library and the maintenance of its streets, Oak Bluffs became its own entity, joining the other four towns of the island (Edgartown, Tisbury, Gay Head and Chilmark). The town name, with little credibility to it being a city, was changed to Oak Bluffs on January 25, 1907. Oak Bluffs remains the only town in the commonwealth of Massachusetts to successfully secede.

BLACK CITIZENS

Records of black people on Martha's Vineyard Island began in 1703. Documents identified by Jacqueline Lois Jones Holland (October 25, 1925–August 15, 2007), who was one of the first to write about them, describe black people as live-in servants who took care of homes and families and mariners who were deckhands, cooks, sailmakers and whale men, one of whom, William A. Martin, became captain of Edgartown-based whale ships in the 1800s.[76]

Freed and runaway slaves had come to the island; John Saunders was one who brought Methodism with him. Black people who lived at Farm Neck supported the vote for secession. Oak Bluffs, becoming a resort for black vacationers at the end of the 1800s, had black entrepreneurs who established successful businesses.

In 1880, a black-owned barbershop, M. Costello's, was located behind the Wesley House hotel in the Campground.[77] Costello's was probably the first black-owned business on Martha's Vineyard. Since then, there have almost continually been bed-and-breakfasts owned by black entrepreneurs, such as Shearer Cottage (1903), some no longer extant, like the Winifred House on Pequot Avenue and Promenade House adjacent to the Oak Bluffs Harbor. Early businesspeople included Georgia O'Brien, Louisa Izett and Mrs. Anthony Smith, who had guest houses on Circuit Avenue for black visitors who couldn't stay anywhere else in the early 1900s. There is a bench in Hiawatha Park near their homes (one of which is the Tivoli Inn) commemorating them with a bronze plaque. Other businesses were George Frye's cobbler shop on Circuit Avenue (1920–68), Ambler

Costello Barber Shop. *Courtesy of the Martha's Vineyard Museum.*

Wormsley's auto garage (1928–46) on New York Avenue (Debettencourt's today) and Pollard's Dining Hall.[78]

Jimmy's Barbeque, on Circuit Avenue in the early 1960s, was owned by the same man as Harlem's famed Jimmy's Chicken Shack in the 1940s. The restaurant Lobster on the Bluffs flourished on Circuit Avenue for a number of years. Some businesses that remain today are Cousen Rose

Gallery (1979), the C'est La Vie gift shop (1994), the Oak Bluffs Inn and the restaurant Biscuits.[79]

The prestigious Martha's Vineyard African American Film Festival commenced in 2002, and the Martha's Vineyard Comedy Fest started in 2010. For the most part, black American people come to Oak Bluffs for vacation.

Rural Improvement Society: 1881

In March 1881, an energetic number of residents formed the Rural Improvement Society of Cottage City, whose mission statement of ninety-nine words neglected to even casually mention its single biggest accomplishment. It elected officers with bold-face Cottage City names, and the membership dues of three dollars were payable at once or in installments. Members were residents and non-residents who held meetings in August, when the camp meetings were in session. In its first summer, the society voted fifty dollars for the "purifying and beautifying of Lake Anthony and Meadow Lake"—a really stinky place—and thanked Joe Dias, the principal of the Vineyard Grove Company, for offering to pay for and plant one thousand larch trees. The next year, the society continued to plant trees (twenty elms along Lake Avenue), and in 1883, it resolved to create public sentiment against unsightly back buildings, backyards and "other offensive sights."

Its biggest accomplishment was voting that a committee be appointed to investigate the subject of a public library. By November, by-laws were complete and requests for books made. In April 1884, a room was rented for forty dollars a year in the Arcade that became our first library. By 1896, it contained 1,422 books, and 3,427 were taken out. It moved to the Eldridge Building (now Edgartown National Bank) in 1907. In the 1930s, it moved to what is now Conroy Apothecary, and of course today, thanks to the impetus of the Rural Improvement Society of Cottage City, the Oak Bluffs Public Library is the treasure on Pacific Avenue whose mission statement reads "Supporting community, building cultural awareness and providing access."

Also in 1881, Cottage City's telephone service started with the first line laid to Vineyard Haven. To use a telephone, one had to go to a hotel or a store, but by 1882, there were seven phones in Cottage City that were called public telephone pay stations. In 1883, we were connected to the mainland by a Western Union telegraph cable. On August 11, 1883, the telephone line from Vineyard Haven to Cottage City was used to get help with the fire that destroyed over sixty buildings on Main Street that night, the most destructive fire in island history.

When I was growing up in the mid-1950s, Bell Telephone employed party lines, where the few people who had telephones in their homes would share them in groups. Instead of today's dial tone, a live operator—almost always a woman—would say, "Operator, how may I connect you?" when you picked up the phone. You would give her the number (or the name) of the person you wanted to speak with, and she would connect you. It was all pretty quaint and civilized—except that anyone could pick up their phone and hear your conversation. This wasn't often a positive development for troublesome kids—like me—whose nefarious plans shared with accessories would be overheard by another mom friendly enough to tell mine and cause extra chores to reduce the amount of free time I had to waste.

In 2013, East Chop's Barbara Block hosted a surprise ninetieth birthday party for her husband, Walter (August 29, 1923–October 31, 2017) with friends and family. Both Blocks, retired schoolteachers, were seasonal visitors since the 1940s. Walt's mom, Rae Block, was one of the nighttime telephone operators in Oak Bluffs back in the 1950s until dial phones came into vogue and changed her career plans. The Blocks were married for seventy-one years before Walter's death.

Telephone poles (with phone, cable and power lines) continue to line Seaview Avenue and the Cottage City Historic District. I agree with C.G. Hine, who said in 1908, "The writer would like to express his disapproval of the telegraph-telephone-trolley poles and wires that line so many public highways to the serious detriment of their beauty; the generation is probably not far off that will wonder why such disfigurements were allowed."[80]

Town Hall: 1882

According to A. Bowdoin Van Riper of the Martha's Vineyard Museum, from 1882 until April 1966, the building facing Pequot Avenue's Hartford Park that is now Cottagers Corner was our town hall. Fitting nicely into the Copeland-designed neighborhood, it was renovated in 1951 with a second story for town affairs and a new police station below. There were vaults on both floors for records and other town valuables and a strongly built cell with a steel-barred door. Over time, it became a fire station—in fact, Oak Bluffs' old 1929 Mack Fire Engine No. 2 called the structure home until Cottagers Inc. acquired it. There's a picture in the August 3, 1922 *Vineyard Gazette* of an architect's sketch of a building captioned "imposing town hall which Oak Bluffs plans to build soon on Niantic Park." The two-storied, multi-columned building with a mansard roof and two-story bell tower resembled the Massachusetts State House, and $75,000 was appropriated for its construction. It was never built. Instead, in the 1960s, architect Winthrop B. Norton designed a new town hall that has since evolved into our police station. The new town hall was constructed at the ferry entrance to town, overlooking the sound and the prettiest park on the planet at a perfect spot…for a hotel. The new building was described by the *Vineyard Gazette* in February 1966 as "the finest example of its kind that the island has ever possessed, and is without question far more attractive and practical than those found in many small towns in the nation." Later, the "shiny, unweathered edifice" was described as looking "Olde New England" on the outside and "the ultimate in modern ideas on the inside."

The *Gazette* reported on the Sunday, April 2, 1966 dedication of the $220,000 building, constructed entirely with town funds following vain attempts of generating federal aid, proclaiming that "Oak Bluffs can go it alone, and we will!"

It is, of course, attractive to no one.

Phoebe Moseley Adams Ballou: 1883

By 1883, Phoebe Moseley Adams Ballou had become one of the first black summer visitors; she worked for the Hatch family in the Highlands. A governess to their children, a housekeeper and a cook, she lived near Bradley Memorial Park with her daughter Caroline until she bought her own house near Call's Market in 1905. Known as S.S. Pierce for the longest time, Call's Market is today Our Market. Ballou's house was next door to Dorothy West's family until 1909, when fire destroyed both. After the fire, the Ballous moved to Bellevue Heights, and today, at least five generations of the family still reside on Pacific Avenue. Caroline and her husband's children included the famed artist Loïs Mailou Jones, Jacqueline Lois Jones Holland's mother. A lifelong Vineyarder, Dr. Holland was an educator and historian who received a doctorate from Fordham in 1973. She published several historical treatises about African Americans, including one for the *Dukes County Intelligencer*. Loïs Mailou Jones (1905–98) was one of the more accomplished Martha's

Vineyard artists. The former Oak Bluffs summer resident has had three books written about her art. Seasonal resident Dr. Cheryl Finley (no relation) of Cornell University published an essay about Jones that speaks to her love for Martha's Vineyard, and the Martha's Vineyard Museum has an oral history recorded by Linsey Lee and reproduced in the book *Vineyard Voices*. One of Jones's works, *Indian Shops, Gay Head*, is in Washington's Corcoran Gallery, and at least four of her paintings, including a self-portrait, are at the Smithsonian Institution.

Today, thanks to her family, several of her works can be seen at the Martha's Vineyard Hospital, known for its world-class art collection.

Eunice C. Rocker

Born in 1847, Eunice C. Rocker had anything but an easy life. It has not yet been easy to be a woman, but to have been black, a Wampanoag descendant and a widow living in Oak Bluffs with nine children at thirty-six years old in 1883 is the definition of challenging. Due to being declared "chronic paupers," she and her family were forcibly removed from the new Cottage City by its constable with several selectmen and sent to the Tewksbury Alms House. The removal included an initial violent attempt to remove the family from their grandmother's home on Lake Avenue outside the Campgrounds, with family and female friends winning the initial assault but losing when reinforcements were called in. A hue and cry ensued, publicly covered by the *Cottage City Star*, nastily accusing the *Vineyard Gazette* of "weeping on the family's behalf." Among the issues—besides the town having had to pay for assistance, medical care and books totaling $155.48—was the assertion that Edgartown should have been responsible for the family (Cottage City had only recently seceded) if not the state. The *Gazette*'s position was that "the notion that paupers can be carted about from place to place until the lawyers find a locality where they can be made to stick is certainly a novel one." The *Gazette* opined, "These interesting people are only alleged paupers, after all. They may have received a trifle of assistance in the remote past, but they claim now to be self-supporting, and there is no law condemning a person to perpetual pauperism because of a temporary lapse from the highest affluence."

The *Vineyard Gazette* was proven right in the lawsuit that followed when the jury asserted there had been improper and unreasonable force in removing the family and awarded Eunice Rocker $450 in damages. While the family continued to cause controversy, on September 19, 1888, Rocker had the foresight to invest in land on the corner of Dukes County and Warwick Avenues where she built the home she died in on August 8, 1911, leaving an estate of $450: $25 in personal property, one lot of land valued at $75, and two buildings valued at $350.[81]

THE FLYING HORSES: 1884

The Flying Horses were brought to Oak Bluffs from Coney Island in 1884 and listed in the National Register of Historic Places in 1979. The ride is a treasure to those of us who grew up with it. My mother took us, I worked there as a ring boy as a teenager, and I took our kids and now our grandkids. Originally called only the Carousel (never a merry-go-round!), the previous Turnell family owners renamed it the Flying Horses in the 1940s. They chose this in a paean to another in Watch Hill, Rhode Island, where horses suspended from chains fly outward as it goes around. Ours is a platform carousel with stationary horses. According to *The Story of Martha's Vineyard*, the word *carousel* is from Spanish and Italian and means "little war." A carousel was used to train cavalry men and horses—they would ride past the revolving carousel and practice spearing one of the rings hanging from the wheel. That's where the idea for the rings came from.[82]

It was initially located next to a skating rink and an eight-hundred-foot toboggan ride and was moved to Circuit Avenue in 1889. Originally built as one of the twenty-five carousels of Coney Island in 1876 (the second oldest), it is the only one with horses carved by Charles Dare. Each horse has a face on the outside and is plain inside. There are two rows of horses: ten large ones on the outside and ten smaller ones on the inside for smaller people. Four chariots are available for elderly people or those who cannot sit atop the horses. It was designed to travel counterclockwise, which makes it easier for most people (who are right handed) to grab the rings. Started by the ringing of a bell (Ding, ding!), each ride is accompanied by waltzes you rarely hear anywhere else. The music was produced by a 1921 Wurlitzer band organ with fifty perforated rolls with about ten songs each that played music similarly to tiny windup music boxes. The prior Stimson wind organ played twelve songs over and over again when I worked there in the 1960s. Along with the sound of the bell starting the ride, my favorite was Juventino Rosas's "Over the Waves." In 2017, the organ was replaced with a hand-cranked piano manufactured in Catalonia, Spain, that plays ten songs.[83]

With assistance from my wife, Karen (and her magna cum laud degree in math), I computed that the horses travel about three miles per hour, certainly "flying" to a five- or six-year-old. For each ride, the ring person (it was only ring boys back when I worked there) loads about two hundred steel rings and one brass one that appears last—catch it and win a free ride. The only person I ever saw catch six rings was Narragansett Avenue's Olivia Steele. Lots of folks say they could catch more—so have those who say they can show you. Operating twelve hours daily during the season, each of three hundred thousand annual rides of fifteen revolutions takes about four and a half minutes accompanied by music that is otherwise timeless. The Flying Horses operate seven days weekly from the day island schools close until Labor Day and on weekends from Easter until schools close for summer. They are conserved and maintained by the Vineyard Trust.

If you want the experience of a time warp, take a ride on the Flying Horses. And once you catch that brass ring, don't let go.

Electricity

Cottage City was the first island town with electricity in 1884 and the first with street lights in 1895. One writer called it the "City of Lights, a fairy land." Cottage City was also probably first in southeastern Massachusetts when, in 1884, the first two generators were fired up in the Highlands. Electric power was provided for street lights in Ocean Park and the Seaview House hotel but was rarely used for interiors of buildings and homes.

Soldiers' Memorial Fountain: Charles Strahan (November 10, 1840–March 24, 1931)

Reconciliation, Redemption and Repudiation

I happened to have been doing some research at the Martha's Vineyard Museum with librarian A. Bowdoin Van Riper one day when an African American couple stopped by on a quest to find out why, of all places, Oak Bluffs, the bastion of black resorts, would have the temerity to host a Confederate soldier's statue. Where was the outrage, they wondered? We assured them it was a statue of a Union soldier; Bo Van Riper pointed out that the prominent "U.S." on the belt buckle proved it—and that the hat was commonplace for both armies. They left the museum library reassured.

The Soldiers' Memorial Fountain statue was placed at Farland Square near today's information booth and was used as a roundabout with a sign reading "West bound cars go to the right, blow your horn" until 1930, when it became a traffic hazard and was moved to its location near the ferry terminal. Arriving unpainted in 1891, the zinc statue was foolishly painted gray to emphasize ties to former Confederate soldiers by the Oak Bluffs Parks Commission when preparations were being made for the American Bicentennial in 1974—I'm glad the couple hadn't been around when the statue was gray. In 1999, historian Dave Wilson noted the mistake, and it was restored to its original color. The statue was a gift from Charles Strahan—incongruously a former Confederate soldier—publisher of the *Martha's Vineyard Herald*, which began life as Oak Bluffs' first newspaper, the *Cottage City Star*. The *Star* was founded in 1879 with the express purpose of helping Oak Bluffs secede from Edgartown, which we did more successfully than the South was able to. Strahan acquired the paper in 1885, five years after we became independent. He changed the name a year later and sold it in 1900. Frustrated that his home state of Maryland had remained in the Union as others seceded, in 1862, he joined the Confederate army. Wounded by a Union bullet and later serving at Gettysburg, he was twenty-five miles away when Robert E. Lee surrendered in 1865, and he recalled with gratitude the mercy that General Grant had shown. Coming to the Vineyard for his health, Strahan's purpose in gifting the statue was to acknowledge the men on both sides who served and died in the Civil War. With a dollar from each new subscription to pay for the statue, Strahan had to cover the final five hundred dollars out of his own pocket. At its dedication on August 13, 1891, Strahan said,

> *That this comes from one who once wore gray I trust will add significance to the fact that we are once more a union of Americans, a union which endears with equal honor the citizen of Georgia with the citizen of Maine; that Massachusetts and South Carolina are again brothers; that there is no North nor South, no East nor West, but one undivided, indivisible Union.*

Inscriptions on three sides honored the Grand Army of the Republic (a fraternal organization composed of veterans of the Union army and navy) and specifically its island chapter. After the ceremony, Strahan hoped veterans of the Union army would offer a tribute to their foes on the single uninscribed side of the monument. On September 4, 1925, the few members left of the Vineyard post of the Grand Army of the Republic provided the fourth plaque: "The chasm is closed. In memory of the restored Union this tablet is dedicated by Union veterans of the Civil War and patriotic citizens of Martha's Vineyard in honor of the Confederate soldiers."

Thanking the Union army veterans for finally paying tribute to those who had fought for the South, Strahan said to the assembly:

> *I bring to you today a message of peace and fraternity, a message in bronze that speaks more eloquently than words. Mark where he stands, the embodiment of patriotism, his arms at rest—emblem of peace, the symbol of the Grand Army of the Republic. Not the star decorated general, whose genius could marshal 100,000 men and lead them to victory, not the sea-bronzed admiral of a navy, the peer of Nelson on the sea—but the private soldier and sailor through whose patriotism, through whose sturdy endurance of the sufferings and trials incident to war, it was made possible to preserve this union, a holy heritage to us and our children forever….As your father and my father stood shoulder to shoulder at Valley Forge and Yorktown, and stood by their guns on the deck of the Constitution and Chesapeake, so the sons of the gray will stand with the sons of the blue, should any foe, domestic or foreign, dare attack that flag.*[84]

Following his speech, the band played "Dixie," and it was reported that "a few rebel yells were heard among the general applause," neither of which would be well received today.

After the years and weather had taken their toll, at a cost of $80,000, the statue was restored, with twenty-two layers of paint removed and replacements of the scabbard and rifle made with casts from authentic pieces owned by the late Bill Nicholson of Oak Bluffs. At its rededication ceremony in 2001, the Reverend John P. Streit from the Cathedral Church in Boston said,

> *This monument was proposed not as an attempt to justify or rationalize the cause many in the South fought for. We should be clear from the beginning that this monument is not about excusing or explaining the grotesque and inhuman system of slavery. This monument was conceived and built as an icon of healing—as a testament to our nation's need to come together again in spite of all the killing, all the casualties, all the destruction that both sides endured.*

In fact, the statue remains the only memorial north of the Mason-Dixon Line to soldiers on both sides. Charles Strahan, with members of his family, is buried in the Oak Grove Cemetery in Vineyard Haven.[85]

In 2019, following requests from the Martha's Vineyard NAACP led by its president, members of the community, including the African American community who did not agree that "the chasm" was closed, mounted a public effort to remove the final two plaques from the statue. Controversy ensued, fueled by social media, letters and editorials in the local press, and in a public meeting, the Oak Bluffs selectmen voted unanimously to donate the plaques to the Martha's Vineyard Museum.

Titticut Follies

Titticut Follies was the name of a documentary film that exposed the inhumane condition at Bridgewater State, once a hospital for the criminally insane. Titticut is the Wampanoag name of the nearby Taunton River and also the former annual show the inmates put on. Importantly, the controversy caused by this film, which was banned for many years in the commonwealth of Massachusetts, is credited for the closure of all similar mental institutions in the state. Of local relevance, Titticut Follies is also the name of the beautiful guesthouse at 37 Narragansett Avenue owned by the Balter family. They bought it in 1981 from Sue Shaw, who inherited it from her mother, Edith Berger. Edith ran it as a guesthouse with no name. When Sue took it over, she was married to a comedian named Bob Shaw, and they made it into an official lodging house. Bob thought it was a wacky business and, being the comedian in the family, named the Oak Bluffs guest house after the documentary.

Titticut Follies, built in 1870, is one of some three hundred homes listed on the 1978 inventory conducted by the Massachusetts Historical Commission. It was once owned by Charles Strahan, the man who gifted Oak Bluffs with the statute of the Union soldier.

CHAPTER SIX

The Oakland Mission: 1895

Massachusetts outlawed slavery in 1783, almost contemporaneously with the advent of the whaling industry, whose racially inclusive meritocracy provided opportunity to free black men, former slaves, indigenous, Portuguese and Azorean men and their North Africa–based cousins of Cape Verde. The Martha's Vineyard economy was bolstered enough by whaling that it provided the financing for the build out of Cottage City. Local abolitionists were in the leadership ranks of the new developments before, during and after the war, when the Oak Bluffs Land and Wharf Company built the new part of town. These factors coalesced in 1895 when Susan Clapp Bradley established the Oakland Mission on Masonic Avenue to help Portuguese immigrants become naturalized citizens. She was assisted by Madison Edwards, a chaplain at the Seamen's Bethel in Vineyard Haven. Edwards, who had taken sick on a vacation, met and befriended Jamaican-born minister Oscar Denniston, the superintendent of the seamen's mission there, who Edwards convinced to come to Martha's Vineyard in 1901. They worked together with Susan Bradley as the mission became a place for Portuguese and Cape Verdeans to attend religious services and learn how to pass the American citizenship test, arithmetic and reading and writing English. After Bradley died in 1907, Reverend Oscar Edward Denniston renamed the Oakland Mission the Bradley Memorial Church in her honor.

The Denniston family. *Courtesy of the Martha's Vineyard Museum.*

Parishioners from several ethnic backgrounds—Portuguese, Cape Verdean, Wampanoag and African American—began attending services at the church, which was recognized as Baptist.

THE BRADLEY MEMORIAL CHURCH

Born on April 5, 1875, in Kingston, Jamaica, Oscar Denniston was remarried (his first wife died) to Medora Curtain (from Jamaica) in 1907, and they had five children, all of whom were born, lived, attended school, died and are buried in Oak Bluffs. The family lived in the building that housed the Bradley Memorial, where a portion of the downstairs was devoted to the church. The Dennistons were a highly educated family. Madison went to Suffolk Law School in Boston; Olive went to Gordon College of Theology and received a master's from Boston University; Dean earned his bachelor's and master's from Boston University; Baron received his bachelor's from Boston University, as did the youngest, Gerald. Dean Denniston was an active contributor to the Oak Bluffs community, serving as vice president of

Union Chapel and a member of the Martha's Vineyard Museum. Thanks to the museum, Dean is one of the featured interviewees left to posterity in the book *Vineyard Voices*.[86]

At times during busy summers, the family used the old Noepe Theater on Circuit Avenue for church services. In 1956, Bradley Memorial was relocated to Pequot Avenue (opposite Cottagers Corner), but it closed for good in 1966.

From 1907 to 1956, this was a building that housed dreams—those of immigrants looking to share our way of life, those seeking spiritual guidance, those considered less than equal—and a humanitarian refuge for them all. Bibles, books and artifacts used by the Bradley Memorial Church, along with correspondence, papers and a host of Denniston family records from 1833 to 1989, were gifted to the Martha's Vineyard Museum in 2008. In a March 1942 editorial, *Vineyard Gazette* editor Henry Beetle Hough wrote, "One does not have to look far away to find things to be proud of when considering the career of Rev. Oscar E. Denniston....He helped bring into reality in his generation the conception of America as a land of opportunity, brotherhood and democracy, not by coming here to become rich, but by coming here to build a church."

The building didn't survive, but the dreams live on.

Portuguese American Club

The 1900s saw the Oak Bluffs economy faltering. As the religious and resort business of Oak Bluffs contracted, land earmarked for development was instead sold as farmland—a proposition welcomed by the newly arrived Portuguese, who had brought farming skills with them. The resulting commerce they established helped increase and stabilize the year-round community. Island-bred Azoreans found Oak Bluffs to be appealing, and by the 1920s, a new neighborhood emerged near Wing Road affectionately called Fayal after one of the major islands in the Azores archipelago. The area included farms on land once owned by Joseph Daggett. Another nearby community called Little Portugal was at the western end of Vineyard Avenue near today's popular Portuguese American Club.

Founded in 1930 as the Holy Ghost Association, the club honors Queen Isabella. Isabella was a fourteenth-century queen of Portugal, the daughter of a Spanish king and the wife of King Diniz. Isabella sold her jewelry to feed the poor during a famine. Legend has it that she hid bread in her skirts, but it reappeared as beautiful roses whenever she was confronted by the stingy king. Every year, the kindly act is remembered by the Feast of the Holy Ghost weekend with a barbecue, games and music. There is also a parade that starts at the Steamship Authority. The Holy Ghost crown of Isabella is held high as a symbol of kindness to the poor. After the parade, there is a celebration with Portuguese soup, food, games and an auction to raise funds. A newspaper article written in 1949 gave credit to the strength of the immigrant Portuguese community that, desiring home ownership, carved out the farms and homesteads, "turning what had been a wilderness into a garden spot and later, a village in itself." They and their descendants, the article continued, "have succeeded to many positions of trust and responsibility in the town's government and business."

The "P.A. Club," as everyone calls it, is not just a social venue but an organization with service as its mission. The club raises funds for charities, scholarships and island people in need. The majority of workers are volunteers. In maintaining the memory of Queen Isabella, the Portuguese American Club has become a net for the needy with the help of a thousand members who care.[87]

The Portuguese have made and continue to make huge contributions to Oak Bluffs.

The Woman in Red

Amid the cool green water of Nantucket and Vineyard Sounds, the red roses and occasional hyacinth of summer are dwarfed by the rainbow of colors of Oak Bluffs visitors and cars. It's not until the fall with the browning of all that was green that the burning bushes (*Euonymus alatus*) and Japanese maples (*Acer palmatum*) distinguish themselves with a last gasp of red to herald the summer season's end.

One Oak Bluffs summer in the early nineties—the 1890s, not the 1990s—that cycle was broken. That was when the "Woman in Red" appeared at the Oak Bluffs Bathing Beach. She was a striking beauty in a red bathing suit with a knee-length skirt, "her stockinged lower limbs exposed as a charm to onlookers." Evidently there was a score of onlookers, and the hearts of men beat faster for the girl whose daring red outfit not every girl could wear. Nellie Sands's Titian red hair, brown eyes and perfect skin elicited jealousy, admiration and the gaze of worshipping admirers. A modest young lady from New York—less than twenty years of age—she seemed unspoiled, perhaps unaware of her beauty. An enterprising man who had left the Vineyard young, found his fortune and returned aboard his own yacht at age fifty, Captain Joseph Raphael De Lamar was the one lucky enough to take the Woman in Red's hand in marriage—upon his contribution to her mother of a half-million dollars, it was said. The two became items worldwide, and Mrs. De Lamar, declared the most beautiful woman in America, was discussed in newspaper articles as one of the four most beautiful in the world. She was often photographed and painted. Alas, upon finding several less-than-discrete letters, after five years Captain De Lamar asked for a divorce. The genteel expressions by both parties of accusation and denial resulted in the two, the multimillionaire and the Woman in Red of Cottage City's dreams, parting. Joseph Raphael De Lamar's estate of twenty million dollars provided half for the Columbia, Harvard and Johns Hopkins University medical schools and half for the daughter of Nellie Sands and Captain De Lamar.[88]

The Automobile Arrives

Five years after the 1895 demise of the Martha's Vineyard Railroad, the *Vineyard Gazette* reported, "Edgartown is in the swim with the other resorts. The first horseless carriage is here. The first to appear is the Locomobile of Elmer J. Bliss, of the Regal Shoe, who brought the vehicle down from Boston Saturday night."

Elmer Jared Bliss was the grandson of whale captain Jared Fisher, founder of the Regal Shoe Company, "one of the greatest concerns of its kind in the world. In his time he served as president, vice president or director of 27 different organizations, including 11 corporations, three banks and two insurance companies."[89]

On Saturday, August 4, 1900, it may have taken Bliss as long as twelve hours to get from Boston to Woods Hole, limited by roads built for carriages and horses. While the first in Edgartown, Bliss's car was not the only car on the island, as the *Gazette*'s Cottage City column reported that another unidentified car had left the island the Monday before.[90]

The first automobile-related fatality was in 1901, when E.A. Mulligan drove a car by a lumber-laden wagon on July 18 and frightened one of the horses, who reared and threw Ariel Scott of West Tisbury out; he died the next day from his injuries. The result was that Vineyard Haven selectmen instituted a six-mile-an-hour speed limit in 1902. After another serious accident in 1904 (also in Vineyard Haven), the *Cottage City Herald* urged

Ladies in car around 1900. *Courtesy of the Martha's Vineyard Museum.*

the town to adopt speed limits; "Automobiles should barely crawl through the Avenues of Oak Bluffs and the Camp Ground. We are not sure that it would not be wise to have a flagman proceed [*sic*] the machine. Speeding 'autos' on our concrete Avenues is dangerous. Roaring lions are not to be more dreaded."

The board of selectmen decided that after August 31, 1905, "Notice is hereby given that after this date no automobile will be allowed to be driven at a greater speed than five miles per hour on any portion of Circuit Avenue between Lake Avenue and the Catholic Church."

In 1903, a Mr. DeWolfe of New Bedford and 30 Narragansett Avenue opened the first "automobile stable," as it was called, on Seaview Avenue in Cottage City. Soon after, H.J. Green, the treasurer of the Vineyard Oak Grove Company, announced in an advertisement "Stabling for automobiles, Central location" for his dealership, also located in Cottage City. In 1906, the *Vineyard Gazette* reported 175 cars on the island, and by 1912, there were three automobile dealers selling cars to islanders. It took until 1919 for people to complain about the roads, largely due to the "suffocating dust" cars created. Few streets were paved; most were covered with crushed scallop shells and wood ashes. William G. Manter of the Dukes County Garage, located at Five Corners in Vineyard Haven, counted 681 cars in 1923, and by 1936, there were 2,108 serviced by the garage.[91]

In 1920, Oak Bluffs real estate impresario Eben D. Bodfish (more on him later) decided to open a restaurant near the Gay Head Lighthouse—and with customers getting there by car, he created the island's first parking lot, completing the trifecta of today's most popular conversations about cars: traffic, cost and parking.[92]

In an article on the centennial of Cottage City's secession from Edgartown in 1980, *Vineyard Gazette* publisher Henry Beetle Hough, describing a 1907 photograph, wrote:

> *Significantly, the only vehicles to be seen on the Circuit Avenue of that time are three horse-drawn carriages, one an open truck. The significance, which hindsight now informs us, lies in the fact that the automobile was fated to bring about the end of the fantasy existence of Cottage City.... At Cottage City, the excursionist and vacationer left the ordinary world behind...the verandas and balconies were for sitting and watching the summer parade of vacationers stroll past. The Avenue itself was more for strolling and shopping than what was now called transportation. In*

Dreamland. *Courtesy of the Martha's Vineyard Museum.*

1907, Cottage City had seven livery stables and no garages. The Tivoli, spick, span, and new...was being advertised as "the new casino" and a photograph—shows its street-side balcony crowded, its banners flying, and only one or two automobiles that can be easily identified in the concourse of men, women, children and horse drawn carriages in the street.

Describing ice cream parlors, salt water taffy and popcorn and reminiscing of promenades, band concerts and rides on the Flying Horses, Hough's piece ended:

There's hardly any convincing proof now that it ever existed, in spite of old pictures and annals. But it did exist, and the coming of the automobile swept it all away, the fantasy, innocence, particular gaiety, and, one should add, inconveniences, too, though they were part of the character and part of the fun. It could not have been possible, but if some millionaire of the time, more farsighted than was ever likely, could have assured the preservation of the old fantasy town, close kindred to the Camp Ground itself, what a living museum the Island would possess today!

Hough would be terribly disappointed to find 27,165 vehicles registered to the island in 2016, over one and a half per home. During the summer of 2017, the Steamship Authority brought 190,735 cars and trucks to and from the island at its terminals in Vineyard Haven and Oak Bluffs.[93]

Phillip J. Allston (1860–1915)

Phillip J. Allston. *Courtesy of Carroll Allston.*

Phillip J. Allston was a chemist at the Potter Drug and Chemical Company, where his work improved Cuticura Soap and Ointment, a product still manufactured. He began coming to Oak Bluffs in 1902, a tradition his grandson Carroll, his wife, Myrna, and their family continues to enjoy passing a fourth generation. The family shared a photograph of Phillip Allston at Town Beach with Carroll Allston's father as a child. In the picture, a biplane offers rides for ten dollars for ten minutes.

Shearer Cottage

On August 28, 1903, Charles and Henrietta Shearer purchased a home overlooking the Baptist Temple Park in the Highlands. Every year, they closed their winter home in Everett from the middle of June until the middle of September and brought the family to their Cottage City home on Martha's Vineyard.

In 1912, the Shearers built a twelve-room home on their property for a summer inn, Shearer Cottage, which was operated in conjunction with a laundry. Shearer Cottage was open to African Americans who were not then welcome at other island establishments.

From its inception, Shearer Cottage more than earned a place in history. Its guestbook, on loan to the Smithsonian National Museum of African American History and Culture in Washington, D.C., has original signatures of the leading people of the day, such as Ethel Waters, Adam Clayton Powell (Sr. and Jr.), Dr. Solomon C. Fuller (the first African American psychiatrist), Henry Robbins (the court stenographer for the Sacco and Vanzetti case), Paul Robeson, composer Harry T. Burleigh, haircare titan Madam C.J. Walker and many, many more.

It's not out of the question that Shearer Cottage may be the oldest black-owned guesthouse, and it continues to be owned and operated by the same family. The current proprietor, Lee Jackson Van Allen, is a direct descendant. Moreover, several family members have themselves earned places in history, like the legislators Herbert Jackson (Lee's dad) and Lincoln Pope Jr. (her uncle).

The one-hundred-plus-year-old establishment is also historically significant for being the first place many other notable black Americans stayed upon discovering Oak Bluffs.[94]

On January 25, 1907, we were officially incorporated as Oak Bluffs, an independent, year-round town of 769 cottages and a population of over 1,000.[95]

Dorothy West

Dorothy West's first year in Oak Bluffs was 1908. Born in 1907, the same year Cottage City was incorporated as Oak Bluffs, West wrote the Oak Bluffs Town Column in the *Vineyard Gazette* from 1967, when it was called Cottagers Corner (the name was changed in 1973) to 1993. On October 21, 1988, she wrote this about the island:

Autumn comes in red and gold layers, and the island calms down to an even tempo. Now there are no amiable crowds to obscure familiar faces. And those faces light up whenever year-rounder's meet, their eyes conveying the assurance that they will nurture each other through the winter months ahead. Here, in this enchanted place, there are very few barriers between rich and not rich, white and not white, erudite and not. Whether it is magic or some other potent that has made these conditions come to pass is something to be pondered. It is my frequent saying that this Island is a microcosm of what the rest of America should be like.

Dorothy West. *Courtesy of the Martha's Vineyard Museum.*

She was brought here by her parents, Rachel and Isaac; her father was a successful wholesale fruit merchant known as the "Banana King" of Boston. The Wests were among the first dozen black seasonal residents, and Dorothy was one of the last members of the Harlem Renaissance art movement of the 1920s who visited the island, including Loïs Mailou Jones, Helene Johnson, Harry T. Burleigh, Warren Coleman, James Weldon Johnson, Isabelle Powell and others who brought creativity with them. In 1926, she tied for second place in a writing contest with future novelist Zora Neale Hurston with her short story "The Typewriter." Today, West's 1965 Smith-Corona typewriter is on display at the Martha's Vineyard Museum and is immortalized in the museum's book *Island Stories*. Her novel *The Living Is Easy*, published in 1948, is my favorite (I have an autographed copy). Her second book wasn't published until 1995, and it was thanks to former First Lady Jacqueline Onassis, who encouraged her to finish *The Wedding*. Onassis, who had read Dorothy's column, was an associate editor at Doubleday and helped get the book published, often visiting with Dorothy at her home in the Highlands. *The Wedding* was a best-seller and was made into a miniseries by Oprah Winfrey starring Hallie Berry. Met with acclaim, *The Wedding* was reviewed as "a triumph" by *Publisher's Weekly*, resulted in a PBS documentary and led to the publishing of her third and final book in 1995. *The Richer, the Poorer* is a compilation of Dorothy West's "stories, sketches and reminiscences" for which she thanked Henry Louis Gates Jr. for encouraging her and the *Vineyard Gazette* and its staff. Dorothy West dedicated *The Wedding* to Jackie Onassis—who died before publication—"Though there was never such a mismatched pair in appearance, we were perfect partners."

Jacqueline Kennedy Onassis wasn't the only first lady to appreciate Dorothy West and her talent; at West's ninetieth birthday party, so large in attendance that it was held at Union Chapel, Senator Hillary Rodham Clinton labeled her "a national treasure." Dorothy West moved here full time in 1947 and stayed until she died in 1998.

The Inkwell

I'm aware of fifty-eight named Island beaches.[96] Martha's Vineyard Island has fifty-three miles of (receding) shoreline, forty-two of which are sandy beaches, and only 37.5 percent are public, the rest private. Some of the public beaches are only available to town residents.[97]

The Inkwell is the only island beach that has been the subject and title of a movie, although not a single frame was shot here. The 1994 feature film, about a young man coming of age in 1976, included such visual malapropisms as sand dunes and palm trees on the beach and a lobster (apparently on Xanax) caught by hand. *The Inkwell* was visitor Jada Pinkett's second film. Historical reports indicate that Martin Luther King Jr. swam there, along with countless other celebrities, film and television personalities. It is easily one of the most photographed beaches island-wide, particularly on social media. Alongside Waban Park, the Inkwell is a great mom's beach adjacent to the Cottage City Historic District lined with benches and wonderful for swimming, sunning and easy socializing.

In Dorothy West's Friday, March 27, 1992 column, she addressed the mystery of the name of the Inkwell—an often-asked question—with this story:

> *For the past few years, Louis Sullivan, President Bush's Secretary of Health and Human Services, has spent his summer escape from the seats of power on this peaceful Island. His walks with a camera trailing him, and a young* Gazette *reporter beside him, have become a tradition. One recent summer, the write-up included a mention of the stretch of water opposite the Sea View Hotel before its conversion to condominiums. Secretary Sullivan was told quite correctly, though perhaps unnecessarily, by some gossiper in the small crowd following him, that that body of water was called the Inkwell, because of the many black Cottagers who swam there. That is not untrue, and it's true that color played a part, but for just the opposite reason. Some 30 years ago it was so named by the most beautiful group of young, black teenagers who rejoiced in being colored (which was the descriptive word then), because most of them didn't look colored—or didn't fit the stereotype of what blacks looked like. They wanted to flaunt or celebrate their origins. Three of them were members, so I know firsthand. Their parents did not share that area; they rode down the Beach road towards Edgartown to the seventeenth or eighteenth pole. It was a secret code known only to the "right" group. But the men in the group used every excuse they could think of to run back to town for some forgotten item—cigarettes, boat schedules or whatever—to sit along the beach wall and enjoy the view. This tale is to reassure those who were offended at the term, the Inkwell. It was a celebration of the teenagers'*

race. When I was a child I was small for my age, and when that was pointed out to me, I stoutly said, "But I'm big inside." And so what these young people were proudly proclaiming was: "I'm black inside."

The diminutive Dorothy West was indeed big inside.

Golf

Henry Beetle Hough's *Martha's Vineyard: Summer Resort, 1835–1935* tells us that a farm in Oak Bluffs was first promoted by Edward Mulligan as the site for a golf course. His view was that the month of May had a favorable enough climate for fans from Florida to come and participate in the activity. The ironically named Mulligan, one of the first to have a car on the island, abandoned his plans when the car was involved in an accident that killed a farmer and sold his interest to Lyman W. Beese, who founded the Oak Bluffs Country Club in 1910. Since then, the golf course has gone through several iterations and name changes due to the combination of interest in the game and finances. Early on, our middle-class vacation resort wasn't as populated with wealthier folks with the leisurely gift of free time, and for many years, it served as Martha's Vineyard's country club.

The original building is where Lola's was, and hole number one is today's number thirteen. Upon a sale in 1953 to James Boyle, the club was updated to include facilities for tennis, shuffleboard and a twenty-eight-by-sixty-four-foot swimming pool with depths from three and a half to nine and a half feet to accommodate divers. The dining room was designed for banquets, receptions, teas and other private functions. In May 1956, according to an article in New Bedford's *Standard-Times*, retired heavyweight boxing champion Rocky Marciano was on hand for the festivities occasioned by the opening of the newly completed facilities and pool hosted by the new operators, the Corkin brothers, who had leased the club. Several officials were in attendance, including state representative Joseph Sylvia (namesake of Joseph Sylvia State Beach), Oak Bluffs postmaster Robert Hughes, Oak Bluffs chief of police Herb Combra and others. In 1962, Ed Barmakian set a club record with a sixty-six that included twelve pars, five birdies and a bogie. According to reports in the *Gazette*, Barmakian led the club for several years.

In 1963, when it was renamed the Island Country Club, a drive by the late Anthony Rebello was greatly assisted when a seagull snatched the ball in the air and dropped it over 360 yards away on the green—which must be the best ball in the history of the club. Coincidentally, his son Todd has scored three holes in one on the course.

A part of a *Gazette* editorial in July 1974 lyrically proclaimed the quandary of the cost and practicality of golf versus the need for a new but not inexpensive course that developers were building called Waterview Farms near Farm Neck. The prophecy proved correct, so even with the pledges of the committed, after spending a half-million dollars on its construction, alas, the next half was unobtainable, and in 1977, its death knell was public.

Fortunately, new operators and owners of the Island Country Club were able to coalesce around a private-public entity in 1979 called Farm Neck Golf Club, a championship club enjoyed by two sitting U.S. presidents and their celebrity friends, many with more recognition than a former heavyweight champ.

Oak Bluffs almost had another golf course near Farm Neck. In 1949, a group of enterprising friends saw an opportunity for what it hoped would have become a new neighborhood around what it had named the Sengekontacket Country Club. From a story and photographs supplied by aunt Emily Robertson, it appears the site for the venture was between Fresh Pond and Major's Cove near Sengekontacket and Lady Slipper Way, south of Pecoy Point. With entrepreneurial zeal, led by the late Sonny Pratt, Charlie Fisher, Warren Coleman and Al Lockhart, a clubhouse was constructed, a pond was stocked with fish, and horses were paddocked to attract investors through the sale of plots of land. Of course, Oak Bluffs had seen its share of similar ambitious plans throughout the late 1800s and early 1900s with names like Bellevue Heights, Lagoon Heights, Oklahoma and Prospect Heights, to mention a few whose reach exceeded their grasp. A difference was, of course, that the ambitious plan for the Sengekontacket Country Club had been embarked upon by a group of long-time Vineyard friends who happened to be black. Another difference was that not only homes were envisioned but also tennis courts and a pool to accompany golf, horseback riding and fishing. Others involved in the planning were the late Coco Lippman and Nat Dickerson, one of the Mariners quartet who for years sang on the *Arthur Godfrey Show*. Dickerson was the dad of the late Natalie Dickerson, a former Martha's Vineyard NAACP president. Natalie's former home at the end of County Road was the original clubhouse for the country club, moved there after the partners, unable to sell as many plots as they wished, ended the project in 1949 and sold the land to other friends, the Horowitz family. Attractive promotional

Golfers. *Courtesy of Emily Robertson.*

pictures taken of the project show a tremendous amount of cleared land with the subjects wearing trendy outfits of the era.

On October 28, 1910, the Camp Meeting Association gave Sunset Lake to the town of Oak Bluffs. There may be a more delicate way to say it, but from 1835 to at least 1900, when Lake Anthony was opened to the sea, Sunset Lake was a bathroom.

THE PHIDELAH RICE SCHOOL FOR THE SPOKEN WORD

In 1912, Phidelah Rice and his wife, Elizabeth, opened the Phidelah Rice School for the Spoken Word, a summer school for acting, at Trinity Church adjacent to the Tabernacle.[98] In 1914, the school was moved to Arlington Avenue in East Chop, and a playhouse was added in 1924. From 1914 until it closed in 1940, several buildings were acquired to house fifty to one hundred students per summer, most from off but several from the island. Phidelah Rice was an accomplished actor who had gained a reputation for "monacting," where one person acted out the multiple roles of a play. One of his best-known performances was *Great Expectations*, a play with thirty-two characters during which Rice read for an hour and a half. In 1934, the *New York Sun* hailed Rice as America's greatest monactor after a performance where he played twenty-four parts: "By sheer force of imagination and a magical genius, he made his men and women appear, disappear and reappear on stage."

Rice's reason for choosing Oak Bluffs for such a high level of cultural expression is indicated in a 1914 handbook for the school:

> *Oak Bluffs is an ideal spot for a summer school. With its picturesque cottages, its adjacent bathing beaches, its wonderful blue skies and bluer waters, it resembles a fairly island. The scene on its streets at night might well persuade one that he had happened upon a fete day in some foreign city; Orientals cry their wares, children laugh, carefree pleasure seekers stroll and talk—surely no place could combine a greater variety of attractions.*

The Rices' two-hundred-seat theater was used for the students (many of whom returned year after year) to hone their craft and was filled with patrons nightly during its many seasons. Occupying several buildings, the school included dormitories (Stag Cottage, North Cottage, West Cottage and Sumner Hall) a dining hall (Club House), the school, the playhouse and later, in 1932, a twenty-five-seat children's theater. Rice provided free bus service from the Island House hotel on Circuit Avenue that stopped at the Wesley House and Ocean View Hotel. Tickets were $1.50 for evenings that included art exhibits, musical recitals during intermissions and cold drinks served at a refreshment stand. *Vineyard Gazette* editor Henry Beetle Hough was a big fan of the theater, writing, "In the early part of summer one would drive to the playhouse before twilight and see the sunset glow in the sky during the first intermission."

It was in Rice's Sumner Hall that Clara Smith's ultimately unsolved murder occurred on the night of June 29, 1940, when the nation was exiting the Depression and the war was heating up in Europe. After this confluence of events, *No Time for Comedy* (ironically popularized by the Vineyard's Katherine Cornell on Broadway) became the last show for the Phidelah Rice School of the Spoken Word's summer theater. Today, the nationally renowned Oak Bluffs school and theater remains in memory only.

A forerunner of what today is called summer stock, Phidelah Rice's was one of the earliest professional summer theaters in the United States.

The Arcade: Blind Nathan

A constant on Oak Bluffs' Circuit Avenue is the Arcade, our first commercial building. Designed by Samuel Pratt and built in 1867 for $6,000, it once housed our first library. Over the years, it's been home to a list of establishments, mostly iconic ice cream fountain stands with a marble counter. The unique structure today houses the popular eatery Sharky's Cantina on one side and the Locker Room, a sports memorabilia store, on the other. An old (undated) New Bedford newspaper clipping quoted a story from the *Vineyard Gazette* about Nathan Ahearn, an Oak Bluffs character. Blind from birth, Ahearn was a lay preacher of the Baptist church. He was listed as indigent by the state of Massachusetts and a resident of West Tisbury in October 1843, when he must have been twenty. Early on, he made a living making brooms, but later in life, he became famous as "Uncle Nathan" or "Blind Nathan." He sold popcorn, candy and sweets from his green market basket on the ball courts, beaches and streets of Oak Bluffs. Unable to traverse the town easily in his later years, Blind Nathan was most

Uncle Nathan. *Courtesy of the Martha's Vineyard Museum.*

often ensconced at the Arcade, where he sat on a small stool next-door and in front of Perry's cigar store. His plaintive cry "popcorn, sweet chocolate, chewing gum" endeared him to all as he became a "much loved, picturesque figure." He wrote a poem entitled "Uncle Nathan to His Friends":

> *Hold your dimes, for I am coming, coming slow but sure,*
> *With my chocolate and corn-bars, fresh and crisp and pure;*
> *I am blind but am no beggar, Doing what I can;*
> *Help me, ye who love the master, help me be a man.*

Uncle Nathan, memorialized by a postcard, died at the age of ninety in 1913. The Arcade was listed in the National Register as an individual property on August 5, 1994.[99]

CHAPTER SEVEN

DIVERSIONS

Constructed largely between 1866 and 1874, in the Victorian era (1837–1901), the Cottage City development was an anomaly compared with the mores of the period[100]—and all the more so given that the new resort had been built as a result of the success of the religious Campground earlier in 1835. Arriving visitors were amazed. "Having been transported from the mundane world into a fairyland, the shock of a miniature city dedicated to joy, pervasive religious feeling, nature, and social density permeated the new decade, even with the resort's blatantly commercial edge."[101]

The hyperbole was about our water, sea breezes, gingerbread cottages, religious freedom—and diversions. Built specifically as a seaside summer watering place, Cottage City was one of the first generally affordable resorts for the middle class. When they chose to take a break from real life in America, they took advantage of all the general frivolity that only Oak Bluffs could provide.

The halcyon days of Cottage City included a colorful array of diversions and activities, few of which remain. With close to a mile of wood-planked boardwalk from the Highlands in East Chop, along the front of today's Oak Bluffs Harbor and down to the Inkwell, "bluffing" was the activity of moonlight strolling to Lover's Rock in the 1870s. Bands played a song called "The Oak Bluffs Galop," written by Etta Godfrey in 1872. In 1873, there were trotters racing at Girdlestone Park, where the Martha's Vineyard

Regional High School is today, with bicycle races held between the horse races. Roque, the upscale version of croquet, was played in Waban Park on clay courts, and Ocean Park hosted bocce games. The Vineyard Skating Rink, built by Worcester founder Samuel Winslow (who invented an improved roller skate), graced the north bluff from 1878 to 1892 before it burned down, and an eight-hundred-foot wooden toboggan ride was replaced by the Flying Horses in 1884 before the latter was moved to its present site. Hockey teams were fielded at the skating rink using roller skates instead of ice skates. Some establishments provided such arcane amusements as saltwater baths, tearooms and arcades with games of skill and chance—recreational activities for a seasonal crowd.

Whispered reports told of the less savory pursuit of prostitution in and around Lagoon Heights at the Reid Hotel that, if true, certainly helped earn us our honky tonk moniker and hearken the Rolling Stones song "Honky Tonk Woman."

The Tivoli Ballroom

Originally called the Cottage City Casino, the Tivoli opened in 1901. Along with big bands, the promoters at the Tivoli brought the public midget and bear fighting, dancing and boxing. There were shops beneath its second-floor ballroom: Harry George's Waterfront Ice Cream Parlor, Whiting's Milk Store, a baggage express counter and taxi stand, a souvenir shop and a shooting gallery that shared space with a restaurant. The name came from the Tivoli Gardens, a famous amusement park in Copenhagen where similar diversions were offered. From 1915 to 1931, piano player, composer and bandleader Will Hardy brought his six-piece Novelty Orchestra from Worcester and placed the Tivoli on the map as a prime spot for traveling dance bands and orchestras. As a composer, Hardy wrote and performed such songs as "Vineyard Isle," "That Wonderful Island of Mine," "Here Comes the *Sankaty*, with My Best Girl on Board" and the endearing all-time favorite "Tivoli Girl." In 2014, his grandson Sterling Smith donated fourteen booklets of sheet music, eleven original music manuscripts and photographs of Hardy and the ballroom to the Martha's Vineyard Museum. In the late 1950s and early 1960s, the Tivoli was used for teenage dances and basketball. The Tivoli was torn down in 1964 and replaced with a town hall that, in 2000, became the Oak Bluffs police headquarters. The Tivoli name lives on as an inn on Circuit Avenue, the

The Tivoli. *Courtesy of the Martha's Vineyard Museum.*

license plate of a popular restaurateur and a mid-September Saturday when Circuit Avenue is closed to automobile traffic and open to walkers for the season-ending Tivoli Day Festival.

Dreamland

Opened soon after the Tivoli and for a time a casino, Dreamland had a long history of entertainment. Dreamland began with ballroom dancing upstairs and nickelodeon movies downstairs. During World War II, Dreamland was used as a recreation center for the navy with pool tables and slot machines. The building was employed for a variety of uses over the years, among them as an automobile garage and skating rink.[102]

In the 1970s, it housed the Second Story Cinema, which featured movies with W.C. Fields, the Marx Brothers and similar offerings, but it didn't last long. Today, it's an adult lounge/game room/pizza parlor (the Loft) following a time as an event/performance hall. Bowling alleys lined Oak Bluffs Avenue, bracketing Dreamland. Pool and billiard parlors were throughout town, including one at Cooper A. Gilkes's Billiard and Pool Parlors at the Island House Annex, according to an ad in a 1910 island directory. There were piers and rafts at the town beaches and paddle boats at Sunset Lake that Joe Pina operated after buying them from the 1939 World's Fair.[103]

The busy summer of 1908 in Cottage City's second year as the Town of Oak Bluffs ended that Labor Day weekend with balloons over Lake Anthony—sponsored by the Wesley House Hotel—and fireworks that evening with The Banda Rosa playing music during the display. Oak Bluffs was the hotel town, the beach town, the first with electric lights, with movies, a skating rink, a carousel, a bowling alley, a dancehall, horses, bikes and cars. America's Great Watering Place had risen to the occasion, providing visitors and homeowners with diversions generally unavailable to America's burgeoning middle class as it rapidly replaced the "Cottage City" signs with the "Oak Bluffs" signs identifying many establishments. Newspaper reports indicated that in the rush to recreate, the enthusiasm for the new and spectacular left something out: there was no nostalgia for the old days. Summertime in Oak Bluffs was exciting with the best of its days ahead.[104]

Today, Oak Bluffs hosts a pirate ship, fishing by the Skipper and My Brother's Charter. Sweets and treats are widely available. Ryan's Amusements is the island's only game room. Giordano's Restaurant and Sharky's Cantina are the Vineyard's two most family-oriented restaurants. Oak Bluffs is a town known for the most parks per capita worldwide, and one, Niantic, has an imaginative playground with basketball and tennis courts. Two others, Veira and Penn, host the Island's Little League. A little farther away from Circuit Avenue, of interest to children is Norton Farm, Island Alpaca, Vineyard Youth Tennis, a skate park, an ice rink and our sailing camp, almost all of which are connected by bike paths. Featherstone Center for the Arts and the Martha's Vineyard Camp Meeting Association each have special activities for children, and everyone island-wide appreciates Illumination Night, the Oak Bluffs Fire Department's annual fireworks show in August and the September Wind festival.

Bowling continues at Oak Bluffs' Barn Bowl and Bistro, with creative life-sized photographs of four presidents bowling—right-handed Republicans Richard Nixon and George W. Bush on the right side and left-handed Democrats Harry Truman and Barack Obama (his is autographed) of course on the left wall.

HISTORIC TALES OF OAK BLUFFS

MOVIE THEATERS

In 1915, the Oak Bluffs population numbered 1,245.

The first theater dedicated exclusively to showing motion pictures, Vitascope Hall in New Orleans, was built in 1896 and was long ago torn down. Nonoperational today, Oak Bluffs' Island is the eighth oldest movie theater in America.[105] The first movies shown on the island were in Oak Bluffs under the Bathing Pavilion on the boardwalk and then in Union Chapel. The Tivoli was used as a theater from 1910 until 1915, when the Eagle was built. An ad in the *Vineyard Gazette* announced that Allen P. Eagleston was opening the island's first exclusive theater, the Eagle (named after himself)—an "amusement house of distinction"—with the movie *David Harum*.[106] At one point, four movie theaters operated in Oak Bluffs.[107]

Inexplicably named the Castle Theater in old postcards, it was ultimately changed to the Island Theatre. The Island is one of the largest and oldest buildings in Oak Bluffs and once upon a time held five hundred people as the largest theater in southern New England.

Including the Island at 1 Circuit Avenue, Fred McLennan operated the (then) three Vineyard movie theaters. He shared a story that it took a year to get a thirty-five-millimeter print of the movie *Jaws* (filmed on Martha's

Island Theatre. *Courtesy of the Martha's Vineyard Museum.*

Vineyard) for its twentieth anniversary. Running all summer long, it exceeded the gross revenue of all of Universal Pictures' summer movies. Lead actor Richard Dreyfuss attended one night, and the audience applauded every time he appeared on screen. In a letter to the *Gazette*, McLennan wrote that the "Island Theater was playing Forrest Gump to a sold-out crowd of four hundred waiting to get in. It was five dollars a ticket. Actress Sally Field approached the ticket booth with her kids to see the film, in which she played Forrest's mother, and she couldn't get in because it was sold out."

Hollywood wouldn't go to bed at night until it had the Island Theatre's grosses. The theaters on the "island were second in soft drink sales and would pop over four tons of raw corn every summer."[108]

Structural problems have persisted at the Island Theatre since a storm in 1924 did substantial damage to its roof, according to a 1926 lawsuit.[109] There has been wide discussion that the building was never built correctly in the first place and would not stand up to today's building codes.

The Island Theatre, the once-proud Eagle, was built as a movie theater and used only for that until August 17, 2012, when it showed possibly its last movie, *Sparkle*, produced by frequent Oak Bluffs visitor Debra Chase Martin. Sony film executive Michael Lynton and Professor Henry Louis "Skip" Gates Jr. brought family and friends together for a special screening in advance of its national premiere in Los Angeles. Lying fallow and decrepit since 2012 as a result of the lack of attention by the family-owned entity, the fate and future of the Island Theatre is unclear.[110]

Diversions helped make Oak Bluffs a popular retreat. It is nostalgia that brings so many back so often.

The Herald and the Old Variety Store

It was thanks to the caption of an 1886 sketch in a story by historian Arthur Railton that the old wooden gifts and souvenir structure next to the Flying Horses was proven not to be Shipwrecked Tallman's peanut stand but instead the Boston Herald Building, originally located on Ocean Park across the street from Tallman's octagon.[111]

Like the *Gazette*, the *Boston Herald* was founded in 1846 and was published as a single two-sided sheet selling for one cent. Its first editor claimed, "The *Herald* will be independent in politics and religion; liberal, industrious, enterprising, critically concerned with literacy and dramatic matters, and diligent in its mission to report and analyze the news, local and global."

Herald Building. *Courtesy of the Martha's Vineyard Museum.*

In the early 1900s, the *Herald* printed a historically significant letter from Reverend Leroy Perry (Chief Yellow Feather) about the characterizations of "Indians." An adaptation of the roof of the *Herald* is to be incorporated into the new building replacing the old Old Variety Store.[112]

Owned by the Peters family for over a hundred years until its sale in December 2017, the Boston Herald gazebo does not appear but is at the left in a ca. 1917 photograph with Bert Riggs and Anna M. Cohan, great-aunt of the most recent owner, Jane Peter. The Old Variety Store was the place with the best penny candy money could buy at a time when fifty cents got you fifty pieces of Sugar Babies and Daddys, Mary Janes, Tootsie Rolls, Dubble Bubble Gum, bubble gum cigars, candy cigarettes, Bit-O-Honeys and, as one would painfully learn, the aptly named Jaw Breakers.

The Old Variety Store. *Courtesy of Jane Peters.*

HENRY (HARRY) THACKER BURLEIGH (DECEMBER 2, 1866–SEPTEMBER 12, 1949)

Harry T. Burleigh was a singer and composer who was instrumental in the development of American music. He helped make black music available to classically trained artists by introducing them to the music and by arranging it in a classical form. Burleigh's relationship with Czech composer Antonín Dvořák, whom he introduced to African American folk music in 1892, resulted in the first time a Negro song became a major theme in a great symphonic work in Dvořák's *New World* symphony. Dvořák directed the National Conservatory of Music in New York, where Burleigh became a musical assistant, and proposed that African American and Native American music be used as a foundation for the growth of American music. Burleigh published Negro spirituals like "Nobody Knows the Trouble I've Seen" and "Deep River" and became known for his arrangements that made spirituals a popular genre for concert singers, including Marian Anderson and Paul Robeson, who, like Burleigh, was a Shearer Cottage visitor when he came to Oak Bluffs.

Robeson coincidentally popularized the role of Shakespeare's Othello, and Dvořák composed the *Othello* Overture, op. 93. Equally coincidentally, the late Liz White of the Shearer family produced the play *Othello* at Twin Cottage in 1962 and the Katherine Cornell Theater in 1979. She invested another twenty years making the production into a movie shown for the first time at Union Chapel in 2012 courtesy of the Martha's Vineyard Museum.

Burleigh wrote over two hundred works, including folk and spiritual choral works, solo songs, violin and piano music. His album *Nobody Knows: Songs of Harry T. Burleigh* debuted at number two on Billboard's Traditional Classical Album Chart upon its 2008 release.[113] In a 1927 *Vineyard Gazette* interview at Shearer Cottage, where Burleigh had been summering and composing some of his music since 1917, the reporter wrote, "The only difficult thing about interviewing this singer and composer with the worldwide reputation, is that he is constantly veering away from the subject of his own work to praise that of others."

Helpful in the presentation of infrequent summer concerts on the island, in 1935, Burleigh named a hymn he wrote at Grace Parish in Vineyard Haven "Martha's Vineyard." From 1923 until his retirement in 1946, an annual service of Negro spirituals was held at St. George's Protestant Episcopal Church (in New York) with arrangements and harmonizations by Burleigh, who could sing in English, Hebrew, Latin, French, German and Italian.

Burleigh's life was a creative, imaginative harmony touched with the emotional power of the Negro spirituals. He was not only a pioneer in singing spirituals on the concert stage but was also among the first to commit to paper Negro folk songs that had been handed down orally. Without his work, they might have been lost, as many black people wanted to forget the conditions they had to endure.

Harry T. Burleigh died on September 11, 1949, at the age of eighty-two.[114]

Biplane at Inkwell Beach. *Courtesy of Carroll Allston.*

AIRPLANES: "$10.00 FOR 10 MINUTES"

Oak Bluffs was the first island town with airplanes. On July 15, 1919, two arrived from the navy base at Chatham, one at the steamship wharf and one at the Inkwell. Both were Curtiss Seagulls, seaplanes as we now call them. Ten days later, another landed in Oak Bluffs harbor, becoming the first charter flight by delivering East Chop's Melvin B. Fuller and Myron J. Brown from Manhattan. Both were Wall Street types, and amateur pilot Fuller told the press he was planning to buy the plane for weekend trips. The plane tied up at the Wesley House pier to the applause of bystanders.

At a dinner at the Wesley House hotel, Fuller compared a trip to the island on his sloop, which took four days, with the plane, which took two and a half hours, including refueling in New Haven.

The story was written in the *Vineyard News* by Eugene O'Neill, weekend guest of Priscilla Hand. The following year, his first full-length play, *On the Horizon*, won the Pulitzer Prize for drama. He and Priscilla Hand shared a ride among the seventy-four who took the short flight to see the island from a thousand feet.

The Fuller plane returned to New York that Monday, and three others landed the following day to show the public the new means of transportation.[115]

Prohibition

The Volstead Act banned the sale of alcoholic beverages and created financial opportunity for struggling Vineyard seamen. The waterways between Vineyard Sound and Noman's Land became "Rum Row," and the Eastville neighborhood docks of Oak Bluffs had a new breed, rumrunners who would meet mother ships from the Caribbean or Canada and fill their holds with liquor bottles, cover them with fish and ice, and transport the cargo to New Bedford, Long Island and Circuit Avenue's hotels and bars, where Prohibition was more of a suggestion than an act of Congress. There was no problem getting a drink in Oak Bluffs—one merely visited one of over a dozen of Cottage City's hotels if one cared to imbibe. The Women's Christian Temperance Union (WCTU), begun in 1874 due to concerns over the abuse of alcohol and its impact on families, chose abstinence as its lifestyle. It visited Oak Bluffs each August, and indeed, Calvin Coolidge—before he was president—spoke to the group here in 1919, just prior to Prohibition. Although homes built by the Oak Bluffs Land and Wharf Company (including my family's) had deeds prohibiting drinking, gambling or commerce on the premises, these covenants were widely ignored. The Prohibition period, from 1920 to 1933, could be likened to *A Tale of Two Cities*—in Edgartown, authorities were confiscating, catching and arresting, while Oak Bluffs was partying like it was 1999. Boats of rumrunners and coast guard enforcers were dying in efforts to foment or thwart the results of fermentation. Long before the Volstead Act, distilled beverages had been addressed in Oak Bluffs. The headline of chapter twenty-six of Henry Beetle Hough's *Martha's Vineyard: Summer Resort, 1835–1935*, "Liquor Is a Problem," told the story. When the Oak Bluffs Land and Wharf Company developed the new resort, the Camp Meeting Association lined Circuit Avenue with a fence to keep the sinners out and the reverent in. In 1887, camp leader Reverend E.H. Hatfield engaged spies who were able to purchase liquor just about everywhere.

Stuart MacMackin

I would have loved to have known Stuart MacMackin (October 2, 1914– March 27, 1983).

Edgartown was his winter home; his summer home was in East Chop, but he spent the summer on Circuit Avenue. A wonderful storyteller, MacMackin diagramed the Circuit Avenue of the 1920s, describing in detail the stores, characters, sights, smells and sounds of a time gone by. He wrote about Circuit Avenue's "Monkey Man" with a street organ and a monkey riding on his shoulder who would offer his hat for change when crowds would gather to hear the music. Two other gentlemen performing streetside music were the hurdy-gurdy men who pulled a five-foot-long piano on wheels to the front of hotels, where one would play music that you might hear at the Flying Horses, and the other would work the crowd for coins with his hat extended. MacMackin, a character himself, reported that the Pawnee House hotel had a porter named Jerry (presumably black) who announced himself at the dock when steamships arrived as "porter for the Pawnee" at the top of his lungs in the early 1920s.[116]

EBEN DAVIS BODFISH

One of Oak Bluffs' more colorful characters was Eben Davis Bodfish (August 11, 1869–October 23, 1944). Educated at Bridgewater's State Normal School, where he studied teaching, he taught for a time on the Cape. His first marriage was to Ann Webb, whose folks owned a hotel and resort in Cotuit where Eben began renting bicycles. When Eben wandered off to the Vineyard, Ann sued him for divorce. He worked at his brother's grocery store, Bodfish & Call in Vineyard Haven, in 1905. Pursuing real estate as a career, he often appeared in a shirt and tie with a tall Panama hat and a rose pinned to his lapel. He was one of the first on the Vineyard to own a car. An April 8, 1920 *Vineyard News* story indicated Eben had purchased the Horatio Pease property near the lighthouse to use as the island's first parking lot for a restaurant he planned on opening in Gay Head.

He particularly enjoyed driving, a skill that seems to have escaped his command as evidenced by his frequent trips to Gay Head being reported in the *Vineyard Gazette*'s (perhaps) shortest stories: "Eben was stuck again." Driving around up in Gay Head irrespective of there being a road or not, most often he had to arrange for a team of oxen to pull him out.

In November 1921, at the age of fifty-two, Bodfish married Elizabeth Jewett Legg, the niece of Hamilton J. Greene, a prominent Oak Bluffs citizen—and Stuart MacMackin's grandfather—who owned the Greene's Block Building, where Eben had his real estate office, on Circuit Avenue. Bodfish's office windows were filled with fascinating things, including "scrimshaw, ivory-headed canes, swords for dueling and swords from swordfish, old ship's compasses, horseshoe crabs, Turk's heads and even ship models, some of them inside bottles," as described by Stuart MacMackin.

Although faithful to his wife, he was known as a ladies' man and a great storyteller who kept his favorites written in two leather-bound notebooks. In mixed company, when asked to tell a story, he would reach for one of the books, his wife would say "Not that book, Eben!", and he would smoothly pick up the other one—which held a less-colorful version.

Eben served on the Oak Bluffs Financial Committee from at least 1923 to 1932—and with one of the first cars on the island, he was surely successful in business. Bodfish was vice president of the Vineyard Grove Company, the successor to the Oak Bluffs Land and Wharf Company, where Hamilton Greene was also an officer. Eben owned various properties, including his folks' home, which was bequeathed to him by one of his brothers. His obituary noted that over his seventy-five years, Bodfish had been principal of the Sandwich Grammar School, principal of the Cotuit High School, associated with the summer hotel business, a member of the board of assessors and a director of the Martha's Vineyard Cooperative Bank. A Mason, Eben Bodfish was also a member of the Martha's Vineyard Rod and Gun Club.[117]

Instead of "For Sale" on his signs Bodfish had painted "Ask Eben" or "Lots for Little."

Bodfish was the first to sell East Chop homes to black people, something prohibited by past practice and restrictions that even today remain in certain land and deed documents in Oak Bluffs. Defying the customs of the time evidently didn't result from his sense of justice; rather, he didn't care.

The Highland Property Trust, which succeeded the Vineyard Grove Company, sold property as late as 1944 only to persons "of the white race… of the Christian religion."

I would have loved to hear some stories from his other notebook.

Phyllis Clair Deitz (September 2, 1921–July 22, 2014)

Phyllis Clair Deitz's daughter and three of her grandchildren were at her bedside when she died. Her obituary was titled "Phyllis Deitz, 90, Was an Oak Bluffs Girl at Heart." In many of her own words, she was born in a little brown house on New York Avenue next to the gas station and garage that her dad had built and later sold to Ambler Wormsley, who was black.

Wormsley sold the business in 1946 to Nelson DeBettencourt, whose family still owns and operates it.

Phyllis was a Gilkes, born to Elsie Schwemmler and Cooper Alleyne Gilkes, and married Kenny Deitz, who stole the Oak Bluffs girl away south to Edgartown in 1949. She remained married for fifty-one years until Ken's death. She lived on New York Avenue until the crash of 1929, before which her dad had owned the Dreamland Garage when it operated tours and had a taxi service. She went to the Oak Bluffs School, was a Girl Scout, played a bugle in the drum and bugle corps and was in the 4-H Club. She graduated with ten others at Union Chapel in 1940 and worked at the Old Variety Store next to the Flying Horses.

After graduating from the Waltham Training School for Attendant Nurses, she worked at the Martha's Vineyard Hospital until September 1946, soon after marrying Kenneth W. Deitz.

Phyllis Clair Deitz was survived by many loved ones on and off island. It's remarkable that someone had the foresight to ask her to write down some of the highlights of her life so that she could share her story of being a mother, grandmother, sister, aunt, wife, homemaker and active member of the community.

Romantically, when Will Hardy wrote "Tivoli Girl," he could have been describing the future Mr. and Mrs. Phyllis Claire Deitz.[118] "Every night down to the Tivoli, to the Tivoli we would go; down where the band played so dreamily, oh so dreamily, lights were low. There I would waltz with my summertime maid, as proud as a duke or an earl, and she gave me her heart while the orchestra played, there I won my Tivoli girl."

Reverend Leroy C. Perry (1874–June 26, 1960)

It's only in magical places like Oak Bluff where one might find himself neighbors with a real Indian chief.

My first summer on Dukes County Avenue, we stayed at a house a few doors down from an old man our folks called "Chief of the Tribe." His putting on a feathered headdress for us was a cherished memory to a six- or seven-year-old.

Reverend Leroy C. Perry at times ministered at the Bradley Memorial Church.

In 1928, the Mashpees formed a new Wampanoag Nation with leaders of groups from Mashpee, Gay Head, Herring Pond and other Cape Cod areas who, over two days of meetings, chose Reverend Leroy C. Perry, minister to the Narragansett Indians of Rhode Island, to be supreme sachem.[119]

He was "an outspoken champion of the rights of the American Indian, and a critic of conditions under which some of them lived on reservations." Born in Tiverton, Rhode Island, Perry's lineage extended to the Massasoit tribe, which greeted the Pilgrims in 1620. He died on Martha's Vineyard at the age of eighty-six.[120]

He was chief of the Wampanoags from 1928 to 1960. Reverend Leroy C. Perry, Ousamequin (Yellow Feather), spoke at the Edgartown Men's Club in November 1933 on Indian folklore, something he toured and spoke about at schools and YMCAs around the country. He stressed that the people of his tribe were not "red faced Savages" but a kindly and brotherly people who had been convinced to swap away all they had possessed without compensation. Well-received, it was reported that the chief was an "eloquent, witty and convincing speaker." A letter to the editor in the *Vineyard Gazette* on September 18, 1936, told of a memorial service conducted by the chief wherein he remarked on the times of Thomas Mayhew and Indian preachers Japhet Hannits, Towanquattick and Hiacoomes.

In January 1946, Reverend Perry's second wife, Susie F. Gladding Perry, died at seventy-six at Martha's Vineyard Hospital as a result of burns she received in a fire at their home. They had been married in 1907.

Before Chief Yellow Feather's death (he and Susie are buried in Oak Grove Cemetery) he wrote a letter to the *Boston Herald* stating, "I am sorry that any group of so-called Americans assumes the right to classify the descendants of the 'original aborigine' called, unfortunately, by Christopher Columbus, 'Indians.' We are not and never were Indians. We, here, were Wampanoags." The letter was signed "Rev. LeRoy C. Perry, Supreme Chief Sachem, OUSA MEQUIN, Oak Bluffs."

His obituary in the *Vineyard Gazette* noted he was survived by his widow (evidently his first wife) Cynthia Taylor Perry and three children.[121]

CHAPTER EIGHT

Joseph Sequeira Vera
(July 14, 1928–May 22, 2018)

Reminding one of the early Oak Bluffs abolitionists, Joseph Sequeira Vera used his legal expertise throughout his career to defend the rights of minorities and women, particularly in housing.[122]

Acquired in 1962, his home at 47 Ocean Park is one with many stories. It was originally built in 1868 by Erastus Payson Carpenter, the leader of the Oak Bluffs Land and Wharf Company's six founders. The cost was $12,000 at a time when homes designed for middle-class vacationers were selling for $700. The house was designed by Boston architect John Stevens, who adapted it from a French design, and Joe restored it in 2004.

Joseph Vera (1816–1894), Joseph Sequeira Vera's granduncle, was born on Pico in the Azores and was an owner and investor in the New Bedford–based whale ships *Cornelia*, *Glacier*, *Lottie E. Cook*, *Mars*, *Orlando*, *Rainbow* and *Midas* from 1866 to 1878. His brother Frank Vera (1836–1918), Joe's grandfather, was a whaler for a time but moved to California, where his first vote was cast for Abraham Lincoln. He established a cattle and horse ranch there before selling it and returning to New Bedford after the Civil War. In New Bedford, he was an investor in the whale ships *Charles W. Morse* and *Lottie Cook*. His son Frank Jr. (1874–1959) became an attorney and later a judge in New Bedford, where his son Joseph S. Vera was born.[123]

Joseph Sequeira Vera holding lifetime NAACP membership certificate. *Courtesy of Lynn Vera.*

Frank brought his family to Oak Bluffs in 1929—the year after Joe was born—and bought a house on Pennacook Avenue. In fact, the family has a picture of baby Joe in front of the old bathhouses at Town Beach.

Joe Vera also became a lawyer, earning multiple degrees from multiple educational institutions. In a great story, he represented a man accused of arson who was acquitted fifty years after another defendant of a similar crime who had been represented by Joe's father. Coincidentally, the judge in Joe's trial had been the prosecuting attorney in the case that led to his father's client's acquittal.[124]

Joe Vera was a remarkably interesting man whom I was fortunate to befriend. Chomping on fruits and berries he grew in his yard, I learned that Joe, like his ancestors, had been an accomplished sailor with many racing trophies to show. He fenced in college, remained an athlete and regularly ran in 3K and 5K runs sponsored by the Martha's Vineyard NAACP and the Martha's Vineyard Hospital. In the hospital's Louis Sullivan Race, he placed first among the eighty- to ninety-nine-year-old men at the age of eighty-seven.

A lifetime member of the NAACP, from 1954 to 1970, he practiced law in New Bedford. Joe was modest about his accomplishments. He served as a legislative assistant in Congress, a director of fair housing for the Department of Housing and Urban Development and a commissioner for the Cambridge Human Rights Commission. He was a natural historian who loved Oak Bluffs, and we enjoyed stumping each other on historical facts—although fairly often I was the one who was stumped. I ran into Joe in the post office one day and was delighted to find he didn't know the small park in front of his house on Ocean Park had a name (Landers Park).

Joseph Sequeira Vera left his family and friends, including me, with many warm memories. The house that remains on Ocean Park is a storied home with the heart of giant.[125]

Joseph August Sylvia (August 19, 1892–December 2, 1968)

In season, a burst of color is provided by beach-goers' cars lining Joseph Sylvia State Beach. A "mother's beach," close to the car with shallow water, it's a safe place to play, a great place for picnics and, after two or three in the afternoon when the kids leave for naps, a place for adults to gather over cocktails, conversation and a swim.

It took from 1941 to 1954 for Oak Bluffs state representative Joseph Sylvia to pass legislation for the state to acquire the beach and maintain it in perpetuity. His father, Alberto Augusto DaSilva, was born in Portugal, his mom, Barbara Cardoza LaConceiedo Lewis, in the Azores.[126]

The senior Sylvia had come to the Vineyard as a gardener, and thanks to a strong family work ethic, young Sylvia worked his way through Suffolk Law School. He was elected as the Republican state representative from Oak Bluffs from 1936 to 1966. He was also an Oak Bluffs selectman, and it's due to him that the navy's old airport, placed under the control of Dukes County, became the Martha's Vineyard Airport when he was a commissioner. His serving as an aviator in World War I probably sparked his interest.

Joseph A. Sylvia. *Courtesy of the Vineyard Gazette.*

In 1941, two teenagers experienced a tough passage sailing from the mainland to Oak Bluffs harbor to participate in the Edgartown Yacht Club regatta. Drenched from head to toe and with no money, on their word one of their fathers would reimburse all expenses (he did), Joseph A. Sylvia—the then-owner of the Ocean View Hotel—allowed them an overnight stay, dry clothes and victuals. One of the young men, Torbert Hart McDonald, later became the congressman for Massachusetts's Eighth District.

The other young man was John F. Kennedy, the future thirty-fifth president of the United States, one of three who have spent the night in Oak Bluffs.[127]

Adam Clayton Powell Jr. (November 29, 1908–April 4, 1972)

Adam Clayton Powell Jr. was one of the more famous—and colorful—of Oak Bluffs' several history-making elected officials. The first black person elected to the New York City Council in 1942, Powell, pastor of the famous Abyssinian Baptist Church in Harlem, became the first black New York U.S. congressman in 1945. He called for an end to lynching and Jim Crow laws and advocated for the independence of African and Asian nations. He chaired the House Committee on Education and Labor and helped create legislation that included a minimum-wage increase, educational resources for the deaf, funding for student loans, work-hour regulations and job training. He served until 1970 when, due to a plethora of controversy, he lost the Democratic primary by a small margin to Charles Rangel, who held the seat until 2017.

Here in Oak Bluffs, Congressman Powell enjoyed fishing, clamming and socializing. As a child, his father had brought him to Shearer Cottage. Powell spent his honeymoon here, and in 1937, he and his wife, Isabell Geraldine Washington, bought their house on Dorothy West Avenue at the corner of Myrtle Avenue, which they called the Bunny Cottage after their pet names for each other, Bunny Girl and Bunny Boy. For years, two wooden cutouts of rabbits graced each side of the front doors until Isabell moved them into the kitchen.[128] Their cottage remains in the family and is a landmark on the Martha's Vineyard African American Heritage Trail—and the bunnies have a new home in the Oak Bluffs exhibit at the Smithsonian's National Museum of African American History and Culture.

The congressman is memorialized by the Adam Clayton Powell New York State Office Building, located on 125th Street at the corner of Adam Clayton

Herbert L. Jackson and Adam Clayton Powell Jr. *Courtesy of Lance Pope.*

Powell Jr. Boulevard in Harlem. The nineteen-story building was designed by the late black architect Conrad A. Johnson Jr., a frequent visitor to Oak Bluffs and guest of my father, Ewell W. Finley, the engineer of the project. Completed in 1973, the late Oak Bluffs fisherman Bob Coveney's company supplied the steel for the building. Years of controversy about the building were covered for the *New York Times* by Oak Bluff's Charlayne Hunter-Gault, and it again made the news when President Bill Clinton made his offices there. Hunter-Gault, a well-known journalist, is a history-maker too, having been one of the first two African American students to enroll at the University of Georgia, where she graduated in 1963.

Adam Clayton Powell Jr. said, "I, Adam Powell, may belong to a group of people that some others may think are inferior, but I belong to a group of people that God, omniscient, omnipresent God, God of all power says 'You are my children, and you're the same as anyone else!'"

Isabell Geraldine Washington Powell (May 23, 1908–May 1, 2007) was divorced from Adam Clayton Powell Jr. in 1945. Evidenced by her picture on a playbill poster for the 1929 Broadway African American musical comedy *Bomboola*, Belle, as she was known, was beautiful. She performed in *Harlem* at the Apollo and *Singin the Blues* in 1931. In 1934, Belle was in the film *St. Louis Blues* and the Academy Award–nominated movie *Imitation of Life*. Once a dancer at the Cotton Club, she met Powell and gave up the theater to marry him.

She learned that not all fairytales had happy endings; along with the divorce, she was a breast cancer survivor. Belle became a special education teacher in the Harlem public school system and remained the center of a large social circle of friends in New York and Oak Bluffs until she died. While here, she attended to her flowers and entertained guests, serving a patented selection of adult beverages on her front porch. An avid angler, she loved saltwater fishing and life. Ever quotable, in a *Vineyard Gazette* interview from 2002, she said, "My only problem is I don't have enough room on my calendar for everything I want to do."

Her personal standards included not coming downstairs without makeup "because I have to look at me. I know who I am. I know who I want to be, who until I die, I will always be."[129] She and Dorothy West, who lived up the street from the Powells, were dear friends. She was always the Belle of the ball.

Johnny Seaview

In the late 1940s, the colorful Loretta Balla acquired the Seaview Hotel across from the Inkwell. It had a small canteen that served what we thought were the best hot dogs on toasted buttered rolls in the world. She also once owned the Norton Corbin House but is possibly best known for hiring the beloved Johnny Seaview.

Once a horse jockey, Oliver H. Perry touched many in his life. He was nicknamed "Johnny Seaview," but we called him John Wayne. He was a little guy with a big voice and a big cowboy hat who stopped by our porch, enchanting us with a "howdy Pilgrims" impersonation on his way to work tending bar at the Seaview.

Perry had a wide variety of occupations, including horse racer, tree surgeon, farmer, serviceman in the army and marines, painter and all-around handyman. He was a ladies' man who went out of his way to surprise with roses. Johnny Seaview had a saying he lived up to: "Want to know what the goal of life is? To relieve suffering, create beauty, and make gardens."[130]

Born March 14, 1928, Oliver H. Perry, the man with the big voice and bigger heart, died at eighty-four, serendipitously on December 12, 2012. Boxcars, Johnny Seaview, rest in peace.

Charles H. "Cee Jay" Jones

Charles H. "Cee Jay" Jones was awarded the Congressional Gold Medal on June 27, 2012, by President Barack Obama. The award acknowledged the segregation of his fellow African American marines at Montford Point, a part of Camp Lejeune, in the Second World War. Congressional Gold Medals, along with the Presidential Medal of Freedom, are the highest civilian awards in the country. Since 1776, President George Washington and Martin Luther King Jr. are among fewer than 350 recipients of the prestigious award.

For twenty years, Cee Jay manned the information booth on Circuit Avenue, answering a never-ending stream of useful questions about beaches, bathrooms and breakfast—and, no doubt, thousands of dumb ones centered on "Oaks Bluff," none of which ever caused him to answer with less than a gentlemanly response.

First coming to Oak Bluffs in 1942, Cee Jay moved here permanently in 1989, becoming a popular personality to children and adults alike. Always neatly attired, Jones had a kind word for all, the twinkle in his always-smiling eyes as warm as a hug. He had a knowing wink too that many saw when he asked someone if they'd like to play a little pool. Cee Jay never played a "little" pool—he'd leave that to you while he ran the table.

Born in Winston-Salem, North Carolina, Cee Jay attended Talladega College, moved to Harlem and joined the U.S. Marine Corps

Charles "Cee Jay" Jones. *Author's Collection.*

in 1943. He retired after thirty-nine years of working for the U.S. Postal Service. Having made friends with the children of the children of friends over the years, Cee Jay has been quoted saying "being blessed is better than being rich," a comment only made by someone wealthy with friends. In a *Gazette* article acknowledging the discrimination he faced, he said, "I believe you should enjoy life and stay positive….Negativity will get you nothing. But positivity lessens the pain."

Cee Jay's patented sign off was "ta ta and apple pie" instead of goodbye.

He died on October 9, 2017, at the age of one hundred and is buried in Oak Bluffs Oak Grove Cemetery.[131]

BLACK RESORT

After World War II the Highlands [of Oak Bluffs] residential section was gradually outgrown and summer people started buying homes closer to the beach and the center of town. They were now beginning to live in what had been called "The Gold Coast," the area roughly between Circuit Avenue and the Sound, from Tuckernuck Avenue to Ocean Park….Mrs. Sally Fisher Clark of Washington bought a house near the Browns… followed by Dr. C.B. Powell, editor of the Amsterdam News *and a New York physician. Others followed in rapid succession. These individuals and others of similar prominence never challenged the prominent role of Adam Powell, Jr., leading very private lives on the island. Even Powell led a relatively restricted life here, apparently enjoying the pleasure of fishing and the company of friends more than the flamboyant role for which he was known in New York and later in Washington.*[132]

Oak Bluffs is not the sole (pun intended) vacation spot for American black people. Others included Highland Beach on Maryland's Eastern Shore, which was founded by Frederick Douglass's son Charles in 1893. Idlewild is a resort on a lake in Michigan where, in 1912, Dr. Daniel Hale Williams, the first surgeon to perform open-heart surgery, was one of the first to buy. Cape May, on New Jersey's southern shore, is another such place; in the 1920s, 30 percent of the population was African American. Sag Harbor on Long Island has been a black vacation area since 1947 and has a 170-plus-year-old church that was once a part of the Underground Railroad.

Dr. Adelaide M. Cromwell

Dr. Adelaide M. Cromwell was the first to define Oak Bluffs as a resort for black vacationers. A Vineyarder since 1943, Dr. Cromwell was born in Washington, D.C., in 1919. She went to elementary school with her cousin the future senator Edward W. Brooke in Washington. Earning several degrees from Smith College, the University of Pennsylvania, Bryn Mawr and Harvard's Radcliffe College, she was the first African American instructor at Hunter College and at Smith. She authored several books and has been widely recognized for her outstanding contributions to academia with awards that include a citation from the National Order of Cote d'Ivoire, the Smith College Medal and the Carter G. Woodson Medal (named for the founder of Black History Month) from the Association for the Study of African American Life and History.

Dr. Cromwell died at the age of ninety-nine on June 8, 2019.[133]

The Swanson House: William Melvin Davey

William Melvin Davey (1884–1949) might have escaped attention save for a highly visible and foolish marriage.[134]

Buying the home on Temahigan Avenue in Eastville in 1943 after making a fortune in California real estate, Davey announced ambitious plans for the Vineyard. The *Gazette* reported that he acquired Cedar Tree Farm to raise squabs and planned to ship his thirty-four-foot cruiser from New York to enjoy at his new residence. The tall blond man was a player on the West Coast and was considered Hollywood's "No. 1 Catch," having dated Clarke Gable's ex-wife, Rhea. In New York, he ran with a pretty young thing named Peggy Hopkins Joyce, a blonde bombshell and actress known for six marriages to wealthy men, subsequent divorces, a series of scandalous affairs, a collection of diamonds and furs and a lavish lifestyle. In 1929, Davey married a twenty-year-old silent film actress named Alyce Mills, a dark-haired, light-eyed beauty who divorced him in 1937.

Davey's weakness for a certain type of woman led him to the actually famous actress Gloria Swanson.

Gloria May Josephine Swanson (1899–1983) had already had four husbands. During one of the marriages, Swanson had a widely known, multi-year, torrid affair with the then-married Joseph P. Kennedy, father of a future president. Kennedy took over the management of her finances, which, like the relationship, didn't fare well, and Swanson was said to have lost over a million dollars in failed investments.

Davey wound up the fifth of Swanson's six husbands following one of her shows on New Year's Eve 1945. They were married midway through her performing in a show entitled *A Goose for a Gander* that tanked in New York that February. It wasn't long before William Davey found Swanson was indebted—and for her to find his health was often impaired by his imbibing. The two found themselves in a publicly contentious divorce in December 1948 that included accusations of infidelity.

In the end, Davey's gifts of two star ruby rings valued at $11,000 were not returned, and for his "abandoning" her, the court awarded $300 in weekly alimony that lasted until her next marriage.

Excluding her from his will, Davey died in 1949 with an estate valued at $300,000 (about $3 million today), the bulk of which was given to charity.

Gloria's sixth and last husband (who outlived her), William Dufty, was coauthor of Billie Holiday's autobiography, *Lady Sings the Blues*. The Davey-Swanson house on Temahigan Avenue was sold at auction to a nearby neighbor, the late Oak Bluffs attorney Henry Corey, for $15,100 in 1950 and is still referred to as the Swanson House.

This isn't the only story the house has.

COLEMAN'S CORNER

Led by Eben Bodfish's willingness to sell property to black people, the Coleman family is one of several with homes in the Highlands. One location on Martha's Vineyard's African American Heritage Trail (founded in 1997 by Elaine Cawley Weintraub and Carrie Tankard) is Coleman's Corner, Ralf Meshack Coleman (1898–1976) and Luella Barnett Coleman's (1896–1996) family compound in the Highlands. Ralph Coleman was called the dean of Boston's black theater, having been the first black director of the WPA Theater Project from 1935 to 1939, and Luella—who we all called "Granny"—created Coleman's Corner, a three-plot family homestead acquired from Manuel Gonsalves for $800 in 1944. It is soon to be in its sixth generation of family ownership.[135]

The entire Coleman story is told in Jocelyn Coleman Walton's lovingly written book, *The Place My Heart Calls Home: Stories of a Working Class African American Family from Boston to Martha's Vineyard*.

The Martha's Vineyard African American Heritage Trail has twenty-eight sites as of this writing.

THE SWANSON HOUSE REDUX: TRUMAN R. GIBSON JR.

In *Knocking Down Barriers*, Truman R. Gibson Jr. includes names associated with Oak Bluffs in the 1940s and 1950s. Gibson, an aide to the secretary of war during World War II, served on presidential advisory committees and helped desegregate the military. He was the first African American awarded the Presidential Medal of Merit and part of the legal team that won the *Shelley v. Kraemer* case in 1948, a Supreme Court decision that struck down restrictive covenants—the term used for denying the sale of real estate to minorities. Gibson represented boxer Joe Louis and became acquainted with dignitaries like Adam Clayton Powell Jr.

Truman Gibson first visited Oak Bluffs in 1946 with his wife, Isabelle, and their friend Etta Moten Barnett, a motion picture actress and star of the 1942 stage revival of *Porgy and Bess*. Barnett was the first black woman to sing in the White House thanks to First Lady Eleanor Roosevelt, who had her sing for Franklin D. Roosevelt's birthday party in 1934. For eight years, Gibson and his family rented the house he believed Joseph Kennedy built for Gloria Swanson (actually owned by William M. Davey).

Gibson enjoyed the town, where he socialized with others like Senator Edward W. Brooke, whose first house on Canonicus Avenue was one block over from a former Vineyarder, Suzanne dePasse of Nantucket Avenue.

Suzanne is a former Motown executive who discovered the Jackson Five. She also founded the company that produced *Lady Sings the Blues*, the movie about Billie Holiday's life based on Holiday and Dufty's book. Suzanne's mom is Barbara Brown DePasse, whose sister is Jackie Brown Llewellyn. Jackie's daughter Alexandra Llewellyn Clancy coincidentally bought the Swanson House with her late husband, Tom Clancy.

The Swanson House certainly has more than its share of stories.

HERBERT LORING JACKSON (1908–1978)

The handsome, impeccably dressed Herbert L. Jackson entered politics early, becoming president of his mostly white Malden High School class in 1927. The thirteenth child of a devout Christian family, where all six brothers completed high school and all seven daughters college, Jackson worked at his father's tailoring business, pressing and delivering clothes. Despite his dad's encouragement to enter the ministry, "Herbie," as he was called, tried Suffolk Law School but soon changed to the Massachusetts School of Art, where he studied drama and went on to perform onstage to critical acclaim.

In 1937, he married Doris Pope of the Shearer family. Popularly elected in 1946, Herbert L. Jackson, a Republican, became Malden's first black city councilor and served for twenty-four years. He also served as deputy mayor, president of the council and acting mayor in the mayor's absence. Noted for his untiring efforts on behalf of youth, charitable causes and civic crusades, Jackson improved the quality of life for all of the people in the city of his birth. After his death, Senator Edward W. Brooke read this into the Senate's Congressional Record on October 11, 1978: "Herbert Loren Jackson was not only my friend, but also my inspiration. He charted a new course in American politics. He proved that a black person could be elected by a white constituency on the basis of individual merit and potential."

Today, Doris Pope Jackson and Herbie Jackson's daughter, Lee Jackson Van Allen, is the proprietor of Shearer Cottage.

COTTAGERS CORNER

The picture above the *Vineyard Gazette*'s weekly Oak Bluffs Town Column evokes many positive memories. If you squint, the stylized cottage looks remarkably like Dorothy West's, the original writer of what was called

Cottagers Corner sketch. *Courtesy of the* Vineyard Gazette.

Cottagers Corner until November 1973, when she changed it to Oak Bluffs. West was one of the early Cottagers, the philanthropic organization of one hundred black women homeowners on the island founded in 1956, when there were only about forty African American families.[136]

Through donations and fundraisers, the Cottagers, under the original leadership of East Chop's Maggie Allston, acquired the former town hall and old fire station on Pequot Avenue in 1968. It was called Cottagers Corner and used largely to keep a lot of us busy with activities other than hanging around Circuit Avenue. The Cottagers host various events to raise funds for island charities.

JUDGE HERBERT EDWARD TUCKER (AUGUST 30, 1915–MARCH 1, 2007)

Herbert Edward Tucker, who founded Boston's first black law firm (Cardozo and Tucker), moved to Oak Bluffs in 1960. According to his obituary in the *Vineyard Gazette*,

> *Under Edward Brooke, he was appointed assistant attorney general for Massachusetts. His assignment was to coordinate the financial division of the office. After working on the successful senatorial and presidential campaigns of John F. Kennedy, he was appointed by President Kennedy to be his representative with the rank of ambassador to the Republic of Gabon in Africa. In 1972, he became the Massachusetts commissioner of public utilities.*

Edward W. Brooke (*left*) and Herbert E. Tucker (*right*), January 15, 1965. *Courtesy of Gretchen Tucker Underwood.*

From 1979 until his retirement in 1985, Judge Tucker was the presiding justice of Edgartown District Court.

Judge Tucker served on the board of directors of our Boys & Girls Club, was a trustee of the Vineyard Open Land Foundation and was member of the Martha's Vineyard National Bank Foundation. A widely popular judge, he was recognized by the Martha's Vineyard African American Heritage Trail in 2018 with a bronze plaque on the Dukes County Courthouse in Edgartown, the trail's twenty-eighth site. "While my depositions will have to be fair they must also reflect a recognition of the wrongs that helped to create these problems."[137]

LENWOOD JOSEPH OVERTON

During his visit to Oak Bluffs, Martin Luther King Jr. was unable to meet with *Vineyard Gazette* publisher Henry Beetle Hough for an interview. In a letter to Hough dated September 17, 1961, he wrote, "I am deeply grateful for all your encouraging words concerning our struggle in the south, and for the support that you gave the Montgomery Improvement Association."

King was a guest at Joe Overton's mansion on Narragansett Avenue, where he worked on a manuscript. Senator Royal Bolling Sr. was Overton's next-door neighbor. About King's visit, he later said,

> One morning I heard children's voices in the next yard, and I looked over and there was Martin Luther King Jr. and his kids playing in my next-door neighbor's yard. He was my hero. I couldn't believe my eyes. I had known him a long time back before he was famous, when we were fraternity brothers…but seeing him in the yard, that was something.[138]

Harry Belafonte, Joe Louis, Malcolm X, A. Philip Randolph, Jackie Robinson and other notables were among Overton's houseguests. Joe Overton was a president of the New York NAACP, chairman of a local school board and active in a host of civic causes.[139]

Overton was chairman of the Harlem Residents Joint Community Action Council, which represented sixty-nine local organizations including about ten black nationalist groups. He was the business agent for Local 338 of the Retail, Wholesale, Chain Store and Food Employees Union and achieved wide public attention in 1959 for organizing a successful boycott of liquor stores in Harlem in order to win more jobs and sales for Negro salesmen.[140]

When Fidel Castro came to New York in 1960, in his address to the U.N., he denounced racial oppression. Housed at Harlem's Hotel Theresa, he met with leaders of the Civil Rights movement, including Malcolm X and Joe Overton.[141]

Some black community leaders protested Castro's visit, like Oak Bluffs' Adam Clayton Powell Jr., who told the *New York Times*: "We Negro people have enough problems of our own without the additional burden of Dr. Castro's confusion."[142]

Rally at the Tabernacle

A *Vineyard Gazette* writer, reporting on a July 1962 Civil Rights rally at the Tabernacle, suggested the appropriateness of the venue due to the Martha's Vineyard Camp Meeting Association's support of equality. Roy Wilkins, executive secretary of the NAACP, spoke to an enthusiastic and near-capacity crowd of two thousand. "It is perfectly fitting for New England to be the mother of our movement, because our ideals and the ideals, traditions and history of New England are one and the same."

Speakers included local rabbis and reverends like the Vineyard's Episcopal Reverend Henry L. Bird, who used the occasion to endorse racial intermarriage. Professor S. Ralph Harlow, an Oak Bluffs resident and member of the NAACP's national board, received one of the largest ovations when he said, "I take pride that there are few places in the United States where the principles of the NAACP are practiced so widely as on our Island—in our schools, on our beaches, in our fellowship and in our worship."

Seasonal resident Rabbi Balfour Brickner noted that "segregation and bigotry though far from dead, have lost about all their real vigor and vitality. Their champions fight an unholy and losing war, as in Albany, Georgia." The audience rose and cheered Wilkins's concluding remarks: "The trouble is not that we are moving too fast. It is rather, that the fight came so late. We have been in this country for 350 years. The first Negroes landed here in 1619, so I tell my white friends that if they did beat us to America it was only by twelve years. Lots of white people I know were Johnny-come-latelys compared to colored people."

The rally ended to a benediction by the Bradley Memorial Baptist Church pastor, Reverend William B. Roane.[143]

CHAPTER NINE

THE *DELEGATE*: C. MELVIN PATRICK

C. Melvin Patrick published the *Delegate*, an annual publication that chronicled the accomplishments of African Americans—including Oak Bluffs people—from 1965 to 1985. Mel and his wife, Fanny Patrick, were known for summer parties at their home on Nashawena Park. "When we last met…" is how Patrick introduced each issue, many of which presented

The *Delegate. Author's Collection.*

photographs of the annual Oak Bluffs Tennis Tournament at Niantic Park. A full set donated by the family is at the Smithsonian's National Museum of African American History and Culture. Mel Patrick, born aboard a ship bound for New York from Panama, grew the *Delegate* from a four-page publication to close to five hundred pages of pictures, program and agenda reprints from the year's events and advertising that supported its cost.

LINCOLN G. POPE JR. (MAY 29, 1916–JANUARY 10, 1979)

The featured event in the community was often the Oak Bluffs Tennis Club Tournament each Labor Day Weekend. It was once joined by Althea Gibson, the first person of color to win the French Open, Wimbledon and the U.S. Nationals, precursor to the U.S. Open. Niantic Park was home to the tournament of the club founded by Lincoln Pope Jr. and his wife, Gloria. Pope's grandfather attorney James W. Pope was the second black person on the Boston City Council in 1881. He often visited Shearer

Harry S. Truman (*left*) and Lincoln G. Pope Jr. (*center*). *Courtesy of Lance Pope.*

Cottage with his wife, Mary, and son Lincoln Sr. Shearer Cottage was where Lincoln Pope Sr., who served the Massachusetts General Court, met his wife, Lily Shearer.

Their children included Liz Pope White, Doris Pope (who married Herbert L. Jackson) and Lincoln G. Pope Jr., who became the first black Democrat elected to the Massachusetts House of Representatives.

The Niantic Park tournament, held on Labor Day for over forty years, was a signature event of the growing African American summer community. Among the hosts of celebrities who attended or participated in the tournament, few were as popular as Ed Brooke, who attended most of them.

Edward W. Brooke (October 26, 1919–January 3, 2015)

Edward W. Brooke was Massachusetts's first (and only) black attorney general, elected in 1962 and re-elected in 1964. He was the most renowned of Oak Bluffs' African American elected officials when, in 1966, he became the first popularly elected black senator since Reconstruction. Following his historic election, it took twenty-seven years before the next, Carol Moseley Braun, was elected senator of Illinois. There have only been ten black U.S. senators (most appointed), one of whom became president and was a frequent Oak Bluffs visitor. Today there are two, Cory Booker and Kamala Harris, who have both visited Oak Bluffs and are among six of the ten with connections to Oak Bluffs.[144]

> *I first came to Martha's Vineyard—it's just clear in my mind, that day when I came across on the ferry—with my wife and our newborn child. And we stayed with a family, Lionel and Edna Lindsay. They lived in Oak Bluffs. We stayed as their guests, I guess for a weekend or something. I just thought I'd found heaven on earth. I found peace. It was the first vacation I'd taken since I came home from the war in '46, because I'd started up my practice and had a child and all that sort of thing. And I'd never gone on vacation. I'd go home to see my parents once in a while, but not on a vacation, of course. So it was the first vacation. I never knew it existed. I was in Boston, living in Roxbury, practicing law there, and came to visit them. I had been elected first vice president of the NAACP and he was president, Lindsay was. And he invited me down here. I fell in love with it.*[145]

Edward W. Brooke at Martha's Vineyard Airport. *Courtesy of the Martha's Vineyard Museum.*

When the future senator bought his first home on Canonicus Avenue in 1949, segregation still existed on the island. "It was rampant here," he said. "We couldn't go to the Edgartown Yacht Club, we couldn't go to the country club to play golf. That place over there, The East Chop club, or whatever it's called, wouldn't have us. They wouldn't allow Jews in either."[146] He acquired his second home on Nashawena Park in 1958 with a large building behind it facing Nantucket Avenue that we called the "mansion." Renovating it into a ballroom, he used it for friends and family as the Island Club. His former Nashawena Avenue home today has a bronze plaque identifying it as part of the Martha's Vineyard African American Heritage Trail.

In summer, the slam of the screen door announced visitors before they called out the name of who they came to see.

It was always special company when it was Uncle Ed, or Eddie as the adults called him, arriving with his booming voice, a firm handshake, a kiss or a hug. Reaching the front door first to greet him, I remember laughing and writhing as he picked me up by the stomach and carried me on his hip wandering through the house, looking for my mom, calling, "Millie, where's Skip?" He'd be tickling me at the same time and saying, "Is he as incorrigible as ever?" Seeing my mom, he'd usually put me down on a coffee table or a chair to give her a hug. She'd be laughing, too, and scolding him to stop encouraging me—and telling me to get down off of whatever he'd put me on.

Ed Brooke was a rock star to many of us in the innocent 1950s in the village of Oak Bluffs, where the Allen, Allston, Coleman, Delany, Evans, Finley, Goldson, Gordon, Guild, Hall, Hamilton, Harris, Hayling, Henderson, Jackson, Jennings, March, Margetson, Meacham, Nelson, Overton, Patrick, Patton, Pope, Preston, Rhodes, Robertson, Slaughter, Steele, Stent, Tankard, Usher, Van Allen, Walkers, Wareham, Washington and countless other families and playmates convened to grow up together, basking in the glow of the man soon to be a senator of the United States and who, like us, happened to be black. All these families whose Vineyard homes Ed Brooke visited have similar stories of personally knowing a senator who would write a letter of reference for college or to the draft board for those particularly unsuited for a military environment, even though he was a war hero himself.

Friends with my parents since the 1940s from college at Howard University, the senator knew me nearly my whole life. I played with his much-adored daughters, Remi and Edwina, and learned some choice Italian words from his first wife, Remigia. Upon hearing about his death, I fondly looked back at our correspondence over my adult years thanking me for the contribution to his last political race or apologizing when he couldn't make the opening of my art gallery in Boston. One letter thanked me for some advice about a radio investment he and a client had considered, and another series of notes asked and thanked me for a contribution for his friend Lowell Weicker, then seeking re-election as a Republican senator from Connecticut. Senator Weicker also sent a thank-you note.

After his death, I spoke with Ed Brooke's cousin, author and educator Dr. Adelaide Cromwell, also a longtime Vineyarder who went to high school with him. She said she never knew anyone who didn't like him. He was caring and honest even as a young man and kept friends for life. Originally, he planned to become a doctor, but Dr. Cromwell thought the war changed him. During his time in Italy, he saw firsthand how black soldiers were treated worse than captive Germans. Dr. Cromwell said she never heard him say an unkind word about anyone, and while he was never wishy-washy, he always looked for the positive in people.

Following the election of President Obama, Edward W. Brooke, the nation's first elected black senator and a Republican, was quoted in a Boston newspaper:

> *Like others, I had prayed that I might live to see the first African American elected president of the United States. I was proud, grateful, overjoyed and tearful when the announcement was made. I believed it could and would*

happen, that one day America would elect an African American as their president. I remembered as a child that mothers would often tell their sons that they could grow up to be president of the United States.[147]

Many of us who grew up on the Vineyard shared Senator Brooke's belief. After all, he was our neighbor, a black man who became a senator. It's thanks to Edward W. Brooke and those like him that it never occurred to those of us who summered in Oak Bluffs that you couldn't be a senator—or a president—even if you were black.[148]

LUCY HART ABBOT

If we keep on fighting, we pass on those ideas to our children and to the next generation, and there may be a change.

—Lucy Abbot
Quoted by C.K. Wolfson
Vineyard Gazette, *May 16, 2003*

An unusually nice person with an unusual nickname, Lucy Hart Abbot died in Oak Bluffs in 2009 at eighty-seven.[149]

Her brother Stanley Hart indicated their parents nicknamed her "Billy Lu," an amalgamation of their names, Bill and Lucy. A younger brother, unable to pronounce the words, called her "Bideau," and the sobriquet lasted. Comments commemorating her life came from around the world. Her *Gazette* obituary was entitled "Bideau Abbot: Honest, Giving and True," wherein son Christopher shared that his mom was a lover of music, literature and art, and every house she owned was filled with all three. In her fifties, Bideau traveled to England, took courses at Oxford University and bought a house there. Her grandson Sixten remembered surprising a U.K. passport inspector by her owning a house in Woodstock—with a passport listing her occupation as housecleaner. Another grandson Jesse learned about service, work and generosity from Bideau. Daughter Genevieve knew her mom as classy, strong and independent, loving of her children, caring about causes, generous, bright and beautiful. Grandson Seth remembered her extraordinary decency and "old Yankee values of modesty, frugality, charity, honesty and caring for the downtrodden." The Reverend Father David Bradley wrote from the United Kingdom, "My House is your house,

Lucy Hart Abbot. *Courtesy of Martha Abbot, photograph by Sam Low.*

was her welcome whenever we visited the Vineyard. Whatever she had she shared. This wonderful woman demonstrated the values that all of us should aspire to….She gave everything and asked no reward, never seeking praise for herself." New Mexico's Mary Jane O'Connor-Ropp said, "Bideau was a woman of deep integrity and humility….It was an honor to know her as her pastor."

Lucy Hart Abbot grew up in a Connecticut family of means accustomed to private school in Switzerland and summering in Harthaven. William H. Hart was the first to own my family house and was Lucy's great-grandfather. Her grandfather was Howard Stanley Hart, founder of the world's first ball-bearing company. Her father, William H. Hart, was president of Hart and Cooley. Following divorce, Lucy Hart moved to Harthaven in 1969 with her five children. After bringing home an African American friend who needed a place to stay, her father and relatives in the family enclave insisted that either he or they leave. They did, and Lucy Bideau Hart Abbot began life anew.[150]

In a wonderful tribute, her brother Stanley wrote, "Because she valued integration and equal opportunity, she told my father that he could have the house; she was not kicking Walter Robinson out." Walter Robinson is the man who wrote *Look What a Wonder*, an hour-long gospel opera. The tolerant Lucy's obituary also mentioned her having had friends that included members of the Black Panthers from New Haven and one of the Harlem Globetrotters.[151]

Bideau worked as a teacher, hostess, waitress, bartender and cleaning lady and yet found the means to contribute to countless organizations in cash and in kind. Stanley said, "From the day she left her so-called heritage, to the day she died, Bideau was proud of her convictions and proud of joining a racially integrated and open society. She was her own person for the rest of her life. She believed one lived with one's fellow humans and not above them or apart from them."

Lucy Hart Abbot embodied the spirit of giving in the purest sense, exuberantly, warmly and selflessly.[152]

CILIAN B. POWELL AND JAMES L. HICKS

C.B. Powell was an Oak Bluffs man of moment who was born in 1894 to former slaves, and following his education at Howard University, he became the first African American x-ray specialist. He owned his own lab and was successful enough that in 1935, with a partner, he bought New York's heralded *Amsterdam News*, one of the largest black newspapers in the world.

Powell and his team, including editor James L. Hicks, expanded the paper's coverage to include national and international news and were credited with reporting on the country's racism. Powell was a lifelong Republican who was uncomfortable with the Democratic Party of old that relied upon the

Historic Tales of Oak Bluffs

Left to right: Edward W. Brooke, Mrs. and Mr. Cilian B. Powell and Mrs. and Mr. Kelvin Wall. Reception at the Powell residence, 1963. *Courtesy of Lance Pope.*

segregated South to win national elections. He and Adam Clayton Powell Jr. (no relation), a Democrat, were political opposites, but along with James Hicks, they vacationed as Oak Bluffs homeowners. C.B. Powell's home was on Tuckernuck Avenue at the corner of Waban Avenue.

C.B. Powell sold the paper in 1971 and became wealthier. Suffering from an incurable disease, he committed suicide at eighty-three and left Howard University his house in Oak Bluffs and $2.5 million, at the time the largest single gift to an HBCU.

James Hicks, like most, joined his family on weekends in between rides on the "daddy boat," which arrived on late Friday summer nights and left on Sundays.

Hicks was the editor of the *Amsterdam News* from 1955 to 1966 and 1972 to 1977. Born in 1915, he had a historic career highlighted by an impressive string of firsts, among them becoming the first black American to cover the United Nations. He was also the first black member of the State Department Correspondents Association and the first to cover the Korean War. James Hicks reported on the school desegregation cases in Little Rock and the University of Mississippi. Hicks was educated at the University of Akron, Howard University and the University of Melbourne during World War II, when he won three battle stars and was discharged as a captain. He is known for his coverage of the Emmett Till case, during which he was threatened and physically attacked by angry white mobs. Hicks found overwhelming evidence that should have convicted the men on trial who got away with killing Till.

Widely celebrated, journalist James L. Hicks paved the way for African American journalists before his death at the age of seventy in 1986.

Dr. Kenneth C. Edelin
(March 31, 1939–December 30, 2014)

When I was 12, I watched my mother suffer and slowly die of breast cancer. I witnessed the failure of science, medicine and prayer as her body withered away to nothing. She was only 46. Through the loneliness of being a motherless child, shuttled from relative to relative through the turmoil of adolescence and rebellion, I became all the more determined to be a doctor—a woman's doctor—to save lives and perhaps spare some other woman's son the anguish I had to go through.

—*Dr. Kenneth Edelin*

Over a dozen dignitaries spoke at Dr. Edelin's celebration of life at Boston University on January 18, 2014, including Massachusetts governor Deval Patrick; his nephew Jeh Charles Johnson, Esquire, former Secretary of Homeland Security; Cecile Richards, president and chief executive officer of Planned Parenthood (who read a letter from Gloria Steinem); and past and present NAACP Legal Defense and Education Fund presidents Sherrillyn Ifill and Elaine Jones. His obituaries in the nation's leading newspapers (*New York* and *Los Angeles Times*, *Boston Globe*, *Pittsburgh Courier* and *Washington Post*) told the story of how Dr. Ken Edelin, soon after the Supreme Court decided *Roe v. Wade*, performed an abortion on a seventeen-year-old girl who with her mother requested the procedure at the hospital

Dr. Kenneth C. Edelin. *Courtesy of Barbara Edelin.*

where Edelin was an obstetrician/gynecologist. It resulted in Dr. Edelin becoming the center of a landmark case on abortion in 1973 where he was accused, wrongly tried and convicted of manslaughter.

The conviction was unanimously overturned on appeal, and he was formally acquitted. His book, *Broken Justice: A True Story of Race, Sex and Revenge in a Boston Courtroom*, tells the story.

JUSTINE TYRELL PRIESTLEY SMADBECK (1921–2004)

Oak Bluffs is a rare place where many have contributed to American black history. Uniquely, our richly diverse town has had black history makers who weren't black.

Justine Tyrell Priestley Smadbeck, surprisingly, was a white, Upper East Side New York mother of four who, from 1961 to 1971, wrote seventy-five columns in New York's historic black newspaper *Amsterdam News* using the nom de plume Gertrude Wilson. Her column, White on White, portrayed the Civil Rights era from a decidedly unique perspective—a woman journalist dedicated to social justice. Justine Priestley wrote about the March on Washington, Selma and Montgomery and the assassinations of Malcolm X and Martin Luther King Jr., whom she knew. She was with Betty Shabazz, Malcolm X's widow, and Coretta Scott King in the days after their husbands' deaths. She received fan mail from Langston Hughes, Jackie Robinson and Adam Clayton Powell and was the only white person at Malcolm X's funeral, about which she wrote "touched me more than I can ever say." In her memoir, *By Gertrude Wilson*, she wrote, "It's my fight, too. If one black person is told he can't vote because he is black—I mean, that's my country. One of my countrymen can't have his rights. It's humiliating."

After the 1964 killings of three Mississippi Civil Rights workers, she criticized President Johnson, writing, "How long before we as a nation realize that lawlessness unchecked is lawlessness unleashed?"[153]

When she was the executive director of the Jesse Smith Noyes Foundation, which provided educational grants to minorities, she met C.B. Powell, the publisher of the *Amsterdam News*. She also met James L. Hicks, the paper's editor. She complained to Hicks that the paper presented all whites as racists—"Your paper is just as biased as you're complaining white people are."[154] Hicks suggested she write some pieces expressing her views, and to his surprise, she did. Justine moved

Justine Smadbeck (Gertrude Wilson) at the *Amsterdam News. Courtesy of Arthur Smadbeck.*

here to Waterview Farm in 1974 and founded the Vineyard real estate firm Priestley, Smadbeck & Mone in partnership with her son, Arthur Smadbeck, an Edgartown selectman.

Her book, dedicated in memory of Dr. C.B. Powell and James L. Hicks and published on Martha's Vineyard, includes the inscription, "I wanted more than anything else to be able to see."[155]

Linda Marinelli
(February 27, 1931–January 31, 2013)

Deolinda Gladys Frizado took the name Marinelli from her second marriage, to Charles, whom she married here in 1961. His family owned land at Sengekontacket in Oak Bluffs where they fished and farmed. From a poor farming family outside of Taunton, Linda was the youngest of twelve children. Over the years, she worked as a nursing aid, taxi driver, EMT and fishmonger. She had a bay scallop shucking operation at the farm, but more importantly, off and on with a firebrand style, Linda Marinelli served as an Oak Bluffs selectman between 1986 and 1999. She was quoted in a *Gazette* interview in 1983: "My husband has a favorite saying. He says I could nag the devil right out of hell. What's right is worth fighting for, even if it means chasing the devil right out of hell."

A classic island character, she was self-taught, and in the 1970s, she mounted a campaign for Oak Bluffs to withdraw from the Martha's Vineyard Commission with the notion that "It's communism for people to impose rules on me and I don't want to live in Russia." Later changing her mind, she became the commission's strongest supporter. Drawn to politics, she mounted bruising crusades with a firebrand style in the name of open government. She was elected in 1986 but resigned in a firestorm of controversy in 1988, returned, but with too many battles to record, was ousted from office in 1993. Marinelli was censured by fellow selectmen and reprimanded by the state ethics commission for her behavior. Compromise was not part of her vocabulary. She was elected again in 1996 and served to

Linda Marinelli. *Courtesy of the* Vineyard Gazette.

1999. Linda Marinelli's legacy was a one-woman battle begun in the 1980s proving that Oak Bluffs, not the East Chop Beach Club, owned a piece of harbor-front property. With old deeds and records and an incomplete set of Massachusetts General Laws she bought for a dollar at a book sale, she spent her own money to press the court case. After a ten-year battle, she won a temporary ruling in state land court that was later reversed with a key concession: a public right-of-way through the property to the waterfront. She said, "I believed then, and still believe now that the beaches belong to all taxpayers." Today, the path behind the Oak Bluffs harbor to Jetty Beach is known as Marinelli Beach.[156]

The former Marinelli property at Sengekontacket is today owned by the Land Bank. It is the Pecoy Point Preserve near Pulpit Rock, where Hiacoomes found Christianity, and the memorial to John Saunders, who brought Methodism to Martha's Vineyard.

CHAPTER TEN

Friday, October 21, 1988

Here in this enchanted place, there are very few barriers between rich and not rich, white and not white, erudite and not. Whether it is majic [sic] or some other potent that has made these conditions come to pass is something to be pondered. It is my frequent saying that this Island is a microcosm of what the rest of America should be like. It may be our interdependence. We are an Island cut off from the mainland. Our year-round population is not overwhelming. We learn to thank God for what we've got. We cherish whoever is nearest. If your nearest neighbor is white and you are not, the fact that she is near enough to come quickly if you call, and the fact that her familiar face is more comforting than some unfamiliar face whose color might match your own are what matter most. In any case the heart, and not the eye, is in command.

—*Dorothy West*

Dr. Louis Sullivan was appointed secretary of the Department of Health and Human Services by George H.W. Bush in 1989. Born in Atlanta, with inspiration from his family physician and encouragement from teachers and parents, Sullivan decided to pursue a career in healthcare.

He graduated from Morehouse College magna cum laude in 1954 before earning his medical degree, cum laude, from Boston University School of

Medicine in 1958. After teaching medicine at Harvard Medical School and Seton Hall College of Medicine from 1963 to 1966, he founded the Boston University Hematology Service, where he remained until 1975, holding positions as assistant professor of medicine, associate professor of medicine and professor of medicine. He specialized in sickle-cell anemia and blood disorders related to vitamin deficiencies.

Sullivan was the founding dean and director of the Medical Education Program at Morehouse College, which became the School of Medicine at Morehouse College. In 1981, the school became independent and was renamed Morehouse School of Medicine (MSM), with Sullivan as dean and president. Except for his tenure as secretary of Health and Human Services, Sullivan was president of MSM until retirement in 2002, when he was appointed president emeritus. Morehouse, whose graduates included Martin Luther King Jr., has an extensive footprint in Oak Bluffs.

Dr. John Wilson Jr., a former president of Morehouse, brought his college buddy Spike Lee to Oak Bluffs to visit his grandmother's home when they were attending Morehouse. On another visit years later, they stopped by to meet Oak Bluffs' L. Duane Jackson, a Hampton graduate and architect who ultimately designed the Lee family's Oak Bluffs home.

Wilson, Lee and the late Dr. Kenneth Edelin's nephew, Jeh Johnson, were graduates of Morehouse's class of 1979.

On a Sunday in July 2016, speaking at Union Chapel, Secretary of Homeland Security Jeh Johnson recalled to an appreciative audience the part of *Guess Who's Coming to Dinner* when, queried about marriage to Sidney Poitier by the dad (Spencer Tracy), Joey (Katherine Houghton) said their future racially mixed son would be from Hawaii—and the president, like Obama, who had appointed Johnson.

Later, at a cookout in Johnson's honor when Wilson and Lee joined him to reminisce, it was delightful to see Dr. Louis Sullivan heckle the three younger graduates.

Dreams can come true in Oak Bluffs, like for Jeh Johnson, John Wilson, Spike Lee, Duane Jackson and Dr. Louis Sullivan.

Lola's

The building that housed Lola's was once the clubhouse for the Island Country Club. From 1993 to 2018, Lola's served as an iconic restaurant, music venue and bar that featured parking, a wide expanse

Kathy and Paul Domitrovich. *Courtesy of Kathy Domitrovich.*

of lawn and the most seating of any island food establishment. Owned by Kathy Domitrovich, a woman of Greek extraction, and her husband, Paul, whose family was from Croatia, Lola's held a special place in the hearts and minds of the Vineyard community, black and white, as a destination for entertainment and socializing.

"See you at Lola's" was an early promotional claim that remained in wide use by annual visitors greeting old friends and families. Lola's was home for the largest of parties hosted by African American–oriented media organizations such as BET and *Uptown Magazine.* Oak Bluffs' Cottagers hosted their annual fashion show there, and the Links, Jack and Jill, the Alphas (and other sororities and fraternities), the Partnership and the Girlfriends all utilized the sizeable space for luncheons and dinners.

The Martha's Vineyard African American Film Festival, Simon & Shuster's 37 Ink Publishing imprint's Writer's Brunch, the Advancement Project and others held receptions and events at Lola's, where it was not unusual to see black celebrities from the worlds of publishing, entertainment and sports. Hailing from Detroit and New York with a host of other successful restaurants, even the Domitroviches couldn't have predicted the role they would play in Oak Bluffs history.

Kathy (Lola) developed the Southern seafood menus, and Paul was the greeter who identified birthday boys and girls to their surprise, delight and often feigned humiliation with a sparkler-decorated delicacy as all the diners sang "Happy Birthday," loudly and at times in unison.

How popular were they? It's a much longer story, but Paul Domitrovich became king of one of New Orleans's Mardi Gras krewes in 2003. He was called King Paul until he died in 2017 at eighty-one years old. Lola's was sold to a local restaurateur in 2018, and the name was changed to Nomans.[157]

Clarence LeRoy Holte
(February 19, 1909–January 29, 1993)

Clarence Leroy Holte and his wife bought their home on Summerfield Park (Laurel Avenue) in the Highlands in the 1970s.[158]

From 1952 until his retirement in 1972, he was an executive at the famous Madison Avenue advertising agency of Batten, Barton, Durstine and Osbourne (BBDO). There he developed its consumer ethnic marketing department and became the first to recognize the buying power of black consumers.

Retiring from BBDO, he founded the Nubian Press, which launched the *Nubian Baby Book*, designed to teach black children about their African American heritage. In his *New York Times* obituary, it was noted that Holte had assembled what was thought to be the largest private collection of books on black history and culture, valued at over $400,000. The eight thousand–plus titles he acquired from around the world covered the history and culture of people of African descent in the Americas and Europe. Some of the collection dated to 1690, and it included many first editions. The collection was sold to a university in Nigeria in 1977.

Clarence LeRoy Holte died at the age of eight-five in 1993 and was inducted into the American Advertising Federation Hall of Fame in 2009. Today, Holte's papers are in the Manuscripts, Archives and Rare Books Division of Schomburg Center for Research in Black Culture, part of the New York Public Library.

Signs of Oak Bluffs

There's no known explanation as to why Penacook Avenue is spelled that way (with one *n*) at the Seaview Avenue end and Pennacook (with two *n*'s) at the other. There's no mountain on Mountain Avenue or camp on Camp Street or bridge on Bridge Avenue. There's no hill on Forest Hill Avenue—and not much more forest than on any other street. We have a First Street (it wasn't) and a Second Avenue and a Third Street that are gloriously inconsistent, and as you may expect, Windy Hill Street has neither wind nor a hill. There is not much to see on Lookout Avenue and no pond on Pond View Drive. We have a South Street and a West Avenue but no North or East. Deer Run is superfluous or obvious, depending on your point of view, as is one of my favorites, Old Dirt Road.

My all-time favorite—the one that brings a smile—is the Oak Bluffs street named Goa Way. Ironically, Goa Way was on the way to Della Brown Hardman's home, the last person on the planet who would want anyone to go away.

Della Louise Brown Taylor Hardman (May 20, 1922–December 13, 2005)

"Savor the moment" was Della Hardman's favorite expression. A granddaughter of slaves, she wrote the *Vineyard Gazette* Oak Bluffs Town Column from 1998 to 2005. Della Hardman earned a bachelor of science degree in education from West Virginia State College, a master's from Boston University and her doctorate from Kent State.

In addition to penning the column, Della made a retirement of service to the community. Della was widely honored and awarded throughout her life, and it's kismet that she was able to attend the first Oak Bluffs "Della Hardman Day" before her death. She is celebrated on the third Saturday of July.

In the preface of Robert Hayden's landmark 1999 book *African Americans on Martha's Vineyard and Nantucket*, Della Hardman wrote,

> *When I think of the plight of African Americans on Martha's Vineyard today, I am reminded of the comments of John Hope Franklin in his introduction to* The African Americans: *"it is not that racism has been eradicated, or that its multiple offspring of discrimination, segregation, and exploitation have disappeared. It is that African Americans have learned how better to cope with the forces that operate against them."*

Amen.

Wayne Coutinho (August 15, 1946–June 3, 2002)

Wayne Coutinho was the first person I ever saw dive head-first off of the old pier at Town Beach. That doesn't sound like too big of a deal until you realize that the pier was about eight or nine feet above about six or seven feet of water depending on the tide. And he didn't just dive, Wayne ran half the length of the pier laughing enthusiastically and leaping with abandon, just like he lived, loving the water above all else.

I think Wayne was the first person to elevate the verb "urinate" to the noun "pissah"—the appellation he used to describe just about everything.

We grew up spearfishing around jetties and, with our friend Richie Steele, probably crabbed out Sunset Lake and "First Bridge" by ourselves. Wayne could hold his breath longer than just about everyone, and I was among the faster-swimming kids, so we did pretty well coin diving at the steamship dock. We also worked at the Oak Bluffs Bowling Alley as pin boys, where the pay was a dime per string (game) and tips meant a lot. The alley used duck pins—the short, stubby ones—and balls without holes that were somewhat larger than softballs. Sitting above the pit at the end of the alley, after people bowled, we jumped down and put a foot on a lever to raise metal spikes to place the wooden pins on so the game to continue. With big hands, I could grab two to three pins in each, which was faster and earned bigger tips. While we waited for bowlers to come in—especially on hot sunny days when everyone was at the beach—we entertained ourselves playing poker and hanging out with friends who came by to pass the time.

Atlantic slipper shells (*C. fornicata*). *Author's Collection.*

When those days passed, I went to school, he joined the army reserves, and we stayed friends. He pursued a career fishing after the service. He was a creative cook, often preparing meals at the Martha's Vineyard Rod and Gun Club. Wayne's claim to fame was convincing the state legislature to designate the limpet—which he found a way to cook—as a fish. We used to call limpets "suck-ons;" they're the toenail-looking shells you find at the Inkwell, sometimes called Atlantic slippers.

It turned out that I knew Wayne F. Coutinho almost all of his life—he was also the first person I ever heard use the term "metastasize." Born on the island, he died after a long bout with cancer on June 3, 2002.

Coin Diving

"How 'bout a coin?" was our plaintive cry to passengers aboard ferries from America as they waited at the dock in Oak Bluffs on the way to Nantucket. The two to three dollars we could make in change could buy French fries from Giordano's and a ride with a cute girl on the paddle boats at Sunset Lake. The bigger kids—and faster swimmers—were able to get closest and catch the best booty of half dollars and quarters, while the slower, smaller kids dove for nickels, dimes and pennies farther away. The smaller kids saved coins to buy flippers to increase speed and masks to see those coins missed that sank to the bottom.

Richard Washington was one of the half-dozen original teenaged coin divers who, in 1956 or 1957, after seeing an adventure movie at the Island Theatre with kids coin diving, decided to try it for themselves. Richard is a former commercial abalone diver, and for twenty-eight years until retirement, he was a movie and television stunt man.

Growing up on the Gold Coast and swimming since the age of seven, I was fast. But I was one of the louder but smaller kids, so a slightly older and bigger coin diver, George Giosmas, looked after me since his mom and my mom had been friends when his family owned the Captain's Table.

Coin diving ended after 9/11; no longer is anyone allowed in the water within five hundred feet of ferries.

Chief Eric Blake

Eric Blake has been chief of police for the town of Oak Bluffs since 2003, having joined the department after being a high school football star in 1987. His mom, Eileen Blake (who died in December 2008) was internationally known for Eileen Blake's Pies & Otherwise.

Oak Bluffs is blessed with a police force whose sophisticated approach to law enforcement provides the comfort of safety and security. Chief Blake assembled a professional, educated team of over a dozen officers. With a bachelor's degree (magna cum laude) himself, he made an associate degree the minimum departmental requirement. On the worst day of our lives, we know we'll be treated with respect and care thanks to Chief Blake.

There are many towns with black chiefs of police, but Oak Bluffs' white chief since 2013 has also been president of Martha's Vineyard's chapter of the NAACP.

African Americans at Home on an Island

On April 5, 2005, the tabernacle in the Methodist Campground was declared a national landmark.

On April 10, 2005, the Sunday *New York Times Book Review* featured a rave review of Jill Nelson's book, written by one of Martha's Vineyard's Pulitzer Prize–winning authors, Geraldine Brooks: "Jill Nelson has written a perfect summer book. Years from now, when it is taken from the bookshelf, grains of sand will drop from its ice-cream smeared pages. *Finding Martha's Vineyard: African Americans at Home on an Island* is part memoir, part oral history, entirely engaging."

She was right.

CHAPTER ELEVEN

I just thought I'd found heaven on earth. I found peace.

—Senator Edward W. Brooke

Philip H. Reed
(February 21, 1949–November 6, 2008)

One of over seventy people featured in Jill's book is Phil Reed, a twin to Eleanor Reed and a playmate of ours.

New Yorkers knew him as Councilman Philip H. Reed from District Eight. Constituents remember him as the openly gay, HIV-positive black politician who legislated for open-space parks, gay and lesbian rights and banning racial and religious profiling and predatory lending practices.

Earlier, Phil worked for Otis Elevator—so he knew about life's ups and downs—but he never looked down unless it was to help someone up. He pursued life with passion, enjoying travel, food and fashion. His friends were bicoastal, worldwide and eminently diverse. His dad was black and his mom, Doris, was white, like the parents of Barack Obama, whose election Phil was delighted to see two days before his death.

The *New York Times*' extensive obituary on the life of Philip H. Reed included a picture of him sitting with New York mayor Michael Bloomberg signing one of Phil's bills into law.

Philip H. Reed (*right*). *Courtesy of Eleanor Reed.*

The Bolling Family

Phillip grew up on Penacook Avenue (in the second block from Seaview Avenue), two houses away from ours on Pequot Avenue, which was four homes away from the Bollings on Narragansett Avenue. They lived next-door to the Overtons.

Patriarch and state senator Royal Bolling Sr.'s love of public service became a family tradition. Royal L. Bolling Jr., his eldest son, was the youngest African American ever elected to the Massachusetts House of Representatives, and another son, Bruce C. Bolling (1945–2012), was the first African American city council president in Boston history. There were eleven Bolling kids, so almost every kid in the Gold Coast had a Bolling his or her own age.

The senator, state representative and city councilor were famous as the first-ever father and sons to serve simultaneously in three different legislative bodies.

Bolling Sr. was a highly decorated veteran who earned the Silver Star, Purple Heart, four battle stars and the Combat Infantry Badge. During his political career, he authored over two hundred legislative initiatives, and as an advocate for equal access to education, his work led to the desegregation of Boston's public schools.

The Nelson Family

The Bolling family home is two blocks from the house where the Nelsons live on the corner of Ocean Park and Seaview Avenue. The Nelson family has owned the house, built in 1880, since the late 1950s.

Patriarch Dr. Stanley Earl Nelson, who died at the age of one hundred on September 6, 2004, was an accomplished dentist who specialized in reconstructive surgery. Growing up in Washington, D.C., his study at Howard University Dental School led to a successful practice on New York City's Central Park in Manhattan with patients who included Sammy Davis Jr., Lena Horne and my parents, his friends. Later in life, the completely interesting "Uncle Stan" became the only person I've known who had his own yogi in India.

A'lelia Ransom Nelson (1919–2001), Stan's former wife, was a former president of the Madame C.J. Walker Manufacturing Company; Madame Walker was the first black American female millionaire.[159]

Author Jill Nelson is one of Dr. Stan and A'lelia's daughters, and Stan Nelson is one of their sons.

The younger Stan won the 2013 National Humanities Medal from President Obama and three Primetime Emmy Awards for some of his twenty films. In Stan's 2004 documentary about the African American community on the Vineyard, *A Place of Our Own*, his father says, "We didn't come to Martha's Vineyard, we came to Oak Bluffs."

Barack Hussein Obama and his family did too, even before his elections as senator and president. He became the fifth (after Grant, Coolidge, Kennedy and Clinton) sitting American president to visit Oak Bluffs and the second (after Grant) to watch the annual Oak Bluffs fireworks in Ocean Park in front of the Nelsons' house.

Final Thoughts

There's an Oak Bluff in Manitoba, Canada, and an Oak Bluff Township in Arkansas, neither of which, like ours, has an *s* at the end of "Bluff." There is an Oaks Bluff Drive in Little Rock and an Oaks Bluff on Pender Island in British Columbia. So when someone says "Oaks Bluff," you can tell them where to go.

NOTES

Dedication

1. Ewell W. Finley, PC, projects include, in New York: Throgs Neck Bridge, 125th Street Harlem Office Building (Adam Clayton Powell Building), Schomburg Museum and Harlem School of the Arts; in Albany: Albany University and New York State office buildings; in Atlanta: Hartsfield-Jackson Airport, Martin Luther King Jr. Center and Atlanta Life Insurance Company; and in Connecticut: Mystic River Bridge and Jackie Robinson Middle School in New Haven.

Chapter One

2. Skip Finley, "The Milfin House—History of a Summer Home," *Dukes County Intelligencer* 52, no. 2 (Spring 2011): 14–21.
3. Ibid.; Skip Finley, "Memories of a Second Mom and Endless Days of Summer at Inkwell Beach," *Vineyard Gazette*, May 5, 2014.
4. Railton, *History of Martha's Vineyard*, 245.
5. Foster, *Meeting of Land and Sea*, 44–45.
6. Banks, *History of Martha's Vineyard*, vol. 2, 3.
7. Hale, *Moraine to Marsh*, 17.
8. Huntington, *An Introduction to Martha's Vineyard*, 6.
9. Banks, *History of Martha's Vineyard*, vol. 1, 59–65.
10. Horwitz, *A Voyage Long and Strange*, 371–73.
11. Dresser, *Wampanoag Tribe of Martha's Vineyard*.
12. Philbrick, *Mayflower: A Story of Courage*, 52–55.
13. Murphy, *Gone A-Whaling*, 14–15.

Notes to Pages 21–30

14. Starbuck, *History of the American Whale Fishery*, 170.
15. Wonning, *Year of Colonial American Frontier History*, https://books.google.com/books?id=qZdNCwAAQBAJ&pg=PT194.
16. Famous Kin, https://famouskin.com/family-group.php?name=3103+george+w+bush&ahnum=4870.
17. "Hiacoomes: The First Christian Indian, and Minister on Martha's Vineyard, by Reverend Experience Mayhew, 1727." *Dukes County Intelligencer* 4, no. 4 (May 1963): 76–82. Reverend Experience Mayhew was Thomas Mayhew's grandson.
18. Ibid.
19. Hale, *Moraine to Marsh*, 18.
20. A.C. Trapp Jr., "The First English Settlers of Martha's Vineyard: The Case for the Pease Tradition," *MVMuseum Quarterly* 59, no. 4 (November 2018).
21. Martha's Vineyard Museum, RU 132, Deeds Collection, http://www.mvmuseum.org/collections/EAD_FindingAids/findingaid_get.php?record-unit=RU132.
22. Stewart, *Names on the Land*, 4–10.
23. Wôpanâak Language Reclamation Project, http://www.wlrp.org/project-history.html.
24. Steve Myrick, "Niantic Park Playground Reopens," *Vineyard Gazette*, July 15, 2016.
25. "Niantic Tribe," https://collections.dartmouth.edu/occom/html/ctx/orgography/org0071.ocp.html.
26. Hale, *Moraine to Marsh*, 28–31.
27. Martha's Vineyard Commission, *The Island Plan*, 2009.
28. There are about 429 homes in the Cottage City Historic District listed on the Massachusetts Historical Register and about 315 more in the thirty-four-acre Campgrounds National Historic Landmark District identified as historically significant.
29. American Fact Finder, U.S. Census Bureau, https://factfinder.census.gov/faces/nav/jsf/pages/community_facts.xhtml?src=bkmk.
30. Landry Harlan, "Welcome Solstice, First Vineyard Baby of the New Year," *Vineyard Gazette*, January 2, 2019.
31. For lists of our neighborhoods, parks, ponds, cemeteries, beaches and islands, see https://www.skipfinley.com.
32. Hilary Wall, "Chronicle," *Vineyard Gazette*, September 7, 2017 (reprinted from September 11, 1942).
33. Skip Finley, "For Whaling Captains, Diversity Flourished," *Vineyard Gazette*, August 17, 2018.
34. R. Andrew Pierce, "Sharper Michael, Born a Slave, First Islander Killed in the Revolution," *Dukes County Intelligencer* 46, no. 4 (May 2005): 147–52.
35. Office of the Recorder of Deeds, Edgartown, Massachusetts.
36. Norton, *Martha's Vineyard*, 52–53.
37. According to the 1850 census data of Tisbury.

Chapter Two

38. Abrams, *Black and Free*, 68.
39. Hough, *Martha's Vineyard: Summer Resort*, 35.
40. Dagnall, *Circle of Faith*.
41. Hayden and Hayden, *African Americans on Martha's Vineyard*, 175.
42. Christopher Rowan, conversations with the author, November 21, 2016–January 10, 2017.
43. Mary Jane Carpenter, "Historic Davis Lane House Began Life as a Private School," *Vineyard Gazette*, February 18, 2018.
44. "Tales from the Big House" project by Christopher Rowan (Christine Luce-Norton's husband), see note 41.
45. Hall, *America's Successful Men of Affairs*, 397.
46. Mary Jane Carpenter, "Historic Davis Lane House."
47. *Vineyard Gazette*, May 20, 1870, 2.
48. "Methodist History: Bishop Fought Slavery," The United Methodist Church, August 21, 2013, http://www.umc.org/who-we-are/methodist-history-bishop-fought-slavery.
49. This section was adapted from Skip Finley, "Captains of Cottage City: The Men Behind the Boom of the Bluffs," *MVMuseum Quarterly* 59, no. 3 (August 2018): 3–20.

Chapter Three

50. Arthur Railton, "When Gay Headers First Got the Vote They Changed the Island Forever," *Dukes County Intelligencer* 41, no. 4 (May 2000): 129–37. Railton wrote, "The original song, 'Ten Little Nigger Boys,' later became a nursery rhyme replaced by 'Injun' boys."
51. John Walter, "That Summer Considered a Bygone Year," *Dukes County Intelligencer* 50, no. 1 (August 2008): 14.
52. Weiss, *City in the Woods*, xv.
53. "Robert Robinson Taylor, Architect and First Black Graduate of MIT," African American Registry, https://aaregistry.org/story/robert-robinson-taylor-architect-and-first-black-graduate-of-mit/.
54. Caroline McCullough, "Summer People: Ellen Weiss," *MV Times*, July 18, 2012.
55. Aaron Modica, "Robert Robinson Taylor (1868–1942)," Blackpast, December 16, 2009, https://blackpast.org/aah/taylor-robert-robinson-1868-1942.
56. https://i.pinimg.com/736x/f4/0b/d1/f40bd120ee5482f48bf5ba290844e3c2.jpg.
57. Dagnall, *Circle of Faith*, 104.
58. Ellen Weiss, "City in the Woods," *Dukes County Intelligencer* 21, no. 4 (May 1980): 123–30.

59. Mary Jane Carpenter, "Camp Ground Pink House Is One of a Kind," *Vineyard Gazette*, July 18, 2014.
60. Oak Bluffs Historical Survey, September 28, 1978.
61. Find a Grave, https://www.findagrave.com/memorial/37685614/luce.

Chapter Four

62. "Sea View in Ashes," *Vineyard Gazette*, September 29, 1892, https://vineyardgazette.com/news/1892/09/29/sea-view-ashes.
63. Skip Finley, www.skipfinley.com; Arthur R. Railton, "When Grant Took the Island," *Dukes County Intelligencer* 29, no. 1 (August 1987): 3–25.
64. Lagoon Heights' Marvin Klein and Susan K. Klein, interview, September 1, 2015; *Vineyard Gazette*, May 7, 1971.
65. *Acts and Resolves Passed by the General Court in 1898 by Massachusetts*.
66. Heather Hamacek, "Gone Camping: New Look, New Name for Iconic Wesley Hotel," *Vineyard Gazette*, May 19, 2016.
67. Railton, "When Grant Took the Island."
68. Substantially altered, the Governor Claflin cottage is at the corner of Pequot and Seaview Avenues.
69. Railton, *History of Martha's Vineyard*, 247.
70. Tourist guide published by John F. of Boston, June 1, 1897.
71. A. Pillsbury, "The Martha's Vineyard Summer Institute," *New England Magazine* 6, no. 1 (June–July, 1887): 4–15.
72. Ibid.
73. Railton, "When Gay Headers First Got the Vote."

Chapter Five

74. Oramel S. Senter, "Oak Bluffs: An 1877 Travel Guide," *Dukes County Intelligencer* 21, no. 4 (May 1980): 133–43.
75. Weiss, *City in the Woods*, 113.
76. Jacqueline Holland, "African Americans on Martha's Vineyard," *Dukes County Intelligencer* 33, no. 1 (August 1991): 3–26.
77. Arthur Railton et al., *African Americans on Martha's Vineyard*, special edition, *Dukes County Intelligencer* (October 1997).
78. Hayden and Hayden, *African Americans on Martha's Vineyard*, 61.
79. Alexander Trowbridge, "Black-Owned Businesses Dwindle on Island," *Vineyard Gazette*, July 31, 2008.
80. Hine, *Story of Martha's Vineyard*, 81–82.
81. Arthur Railton, "Widow Rocker, Part Indian, Struggles to Break the Chains of Poverty," *Dukes County Intelligencer* 47, no. 3 (February 2006): 79–90.

82. Clyde L. Mackenzie Jr., "A Cherished Artifact: The Flying Horses," *Dukes County Intelligencer* 47, no. 3 (February 2006): 91–104.
83. Ivy Ashe, "Flying Horses Make Room in Stable for Tiny Catalonian Piano," *Vineyard Gazette*, January 17, 2014, http://mvgazette.com/news/2014/01/17/flying-horses-make-room-stable-tiny-catalonian-piano?k=vg52d5dd7b9de24#sthash.bm81EAUW.dpuf.
84. "Confederate Soldier Honors the Blue," *Vineyard Gazette*, June 5, 1925.
85. Tom Dunlop, "Uniting the Divided: A Civil War Monument in Oak Bluffs Honors Both Confederate and Union Soldiers," *Martha's Vineyard Magazine*, August 2013. Sources for the article came from the libraries of the Martha's Vineyard Museum and the *Vineyard Gazette*; David Wilson of the Soldiers' Memorial Fountain Restoration Committee; and Dr. William T. Strahan of Silver Spring, Maryland.

Chapter Six

86. Lee, *Vineyard Voices*, 162–67.
87. Phyllis Meras, "The Allure of the Azores," *Martha's Vineyard Magazine*, September/October 2012, 42–51.
88. Hough, *Martha's Vineyard: Summer Resort*, 220–25.
89. Edgartown Town Column, *Vineyard Gazette*, August 9, 1900.
90. Cottage City Column, *Vineyard Gazette*, September 6, 1900.
91. Mary Breslauer, "Traffic Report: Thirty Years Ago the Vineyard Towns All Voted to Limit Cars on the Island and That Changed…Precisely Nothing," *Martha's Vineyard Magazine*, May/June 2018, 68–71.
92. Arthur Railton, "Our First Automobile Arrived 100 Years Ago," *Dukes County Intelligencer* 42, no. 2 (November 2000): 74–86.
93. Chloe Reichel, "Not Just Your Imagination, Summer Traffic Is on the Rise," *Vineyard Gazette*, September 1, 2017.
94. Shelley Christensen, "The Shearer Family, Keepers of the Inn," *Martha's Vineyard Magazine*, May/June 2012, 70–81.
95. Weiss, *City in the Woods*.
96. For a list of island beaches, see www.skipfinley.com.
97. Remy Tumin, "A Peek Past the Gate of Key Beaches," *Vineyard Gazette*, August 2, 2012.
98. Stuart MacMackin, "Phidelah Rice School of the Spoken Word," *Dukes County Intelligencer* 24, no. 1 (August 1982): 18–30.
99. Massachusetts Cultural Resource Information System, http://mhc-macris.net/Details.aspx?MhcId=OAK.593.

Notes to Pages 107–120

Chapter Seven

100. Anne Shepherd, "Overview of the Victorian Era," History in Focus, April 2001, https://www.history.ac.uk/ihr/Focus/Victorians/article.html.
101. Weiss, *City in the Woods*, 113.
102. Olivia Hull, "Dreamland Unveils Loft, an Adult Game Room," *Vineyard Gazette*, March 13, 2015.
103. Vaughn Barmakian, "Penny Candy Memories of Oak Bluffs," *Vineyard Gazette*, March 8, 2017.
104. Skip Finley, Oak Bluffs Town Column, *Vineyard Gazette*, August 31, 2013.
105. Graham Opera House, Washington, Iowa (1897); Roxie, San Francisco (1909); Priest Theater, High Springs, Florida (1910); Empress, Vallejo, California (1911); Elks, Middletown, Pennsylvania (1911); Park, Estes, Colorado (1913); Ruby, Chelan, Washington (1914).
106. Advertisement, *Vineyard Gazette*, June 3, 1915.
107. Railton, *History of Martha's Vineyard*, 351–54. The Eagle, the Pastime (which played westerns with Harry Carey and Tom Mix), the Noepe (sold to the Denniston family in 1923) and one at Dreamland; the Strand came along in 1930.
108. Fred McLennan, letter to editor, *Vineyard Gazette*, March 21, 2014.
109. Lillian E. Judkins v. Thomas J. Charette and Others, 255 Mass. 76, December 3, 1925–February 26, 1926. Justicia, https://law.justia.com/cases/massachusetts/supreme-court/volumes/255/255mass76.html.
110. Alex Elvin, "Island Theatre Work Nearly Complete," *Vineyard Gazette*, July 13, 2017; "Overdue Painting Begins at Island Theatre," *Vineyard Gazette*, August 11, 2017; Steve Myrick, "Questions Surface Over Island Theatre," *Vineyard Gazette*, August 17, 2018.
111. Arthur Railton, "Cape Pogue Light: Remote and Lonely, Part Two," *Dukes County Intelligencer* 25, no. 3 (February 1984): 122.
112. Noah Asimow, "Mixed Reviews Greet Plans for Old Variety Store," *Vineyard Gazette*, January 11, 2019.
113. Michael Beckermannov, "Dvorak as Prime Mover, Sitting Duck and More," *New York Times*, November 17, 2002.
114. "H.T. Burleigh Was One of Music's Great Figures, Visited Island for Generation, Composed Some of Work Here, Inspired Dvorak Symphony," *Vineyard Gazette*, September 16, 1949.
115. Arthur Railton, "The Vineyard's First Airplane Arrivals," *Dukes County Intelligencer* 35, no. 1 (August 1993): 35–39.
116. Stuart MacMackin, "I Was a Circuit Avenue Street Kid," *Dukes County Intelligencer* 24, no. 3 (February 1983): 83–109.
117. "Eben Bodfish Dies," *Vineyard Gazette*, October 27, 1944.
118. "Phyllis Deitz, 90, Was an Oak Bluffs Girl at Heart," *Vineyard Gazette*, July 26, 2014.

119. Campisi, *The Mashpee Indians*, 134–36.
120. "Rev. Leroy C. Leroy Perry, Wampanoag Leader," *Newport Daily News*, June 28, 1960, 2.
121. Obituary, *Vineyard Gazette*, July 1, 1960.

Chapter Eight

122. "Joseph Vera Lived Life of Civic Engagement, Volunteerism," *Vineyard Gazette*, May 30, 2018.
123. Amaral, *They Ploughed the Seas*, 150–51.
124. Joe Vera, letter to the author, August 10, 2015.
125. Skip Finley, "Houses Carry Stories in Every Room," *Vineyard Gazette*, June 14, 2018.
126. June Manning, *Vineyard Gazette* Aquinnah columnist and former relative, in discussion with the author.
127. Joseph Chase Allen, "President Kennedy Slept in Room L at Ocean View, and This Is How It Happened, Rep. Sylvia Recalls," *Vineyard Gazette*, December 29, 1961.
128. Hayden and Hayden, *African Americans on Martha's Vineyard*, 35–38.
129. Skip Finley, Oak Bluffs Town Column, *Vineyard Gazette*, June 17, 2016.
130. Brooks Robards, "Johnny 'Seaview' Perry," *Martha's Vineyard Magazine*, July 2005, 12, 28.
131. "Charles H. Jones, Centenarian, Was a Gold Medal Veteran," *Vineyard Gazette*, July 27, 2018.
132. Adelaide M. Cromwell, "The History of Oak Bluffs as a Popular Resort for Blacks: African Americans on Martha's Vineyard," *African Americans on Martha's Vineyard*, special edition, *Dukes County Intelligencer* (October 1997): 47–69.
133. "Adelaide Cromwell, Influential African American Intellectual, Dies at 99," *Vineyard Gazette*, June 21, 2019.
134. Shearer, *Gloria Swanson*, 302–8.
135. Walton, *The Place My Heart Calls Home*.
136. The Cottagers Inc., https://www.thecottagersincofmv.org.
137. Noah Asimow, "Honoring the Legacy of Judge Herbert Tucker," *Vineyard Gazette*, July 2, 2018.
138. Richard Lewis Taylor, Oak Bluffs Town Column, *Vineyard Gazette*, January 5, 2018.
139. Metropolitan Column, *New York Times*, November 13, 1970.
140. "L. Joseph Overton United Council of Harlem Organizations," *New York Times*, August 10, 1964.
141. Cameron Orr, "Following Tradition Started by Fidel, Cuba's New President Visits Harlem," *People's World*, October 4, 2018, https://www.peoplesworld.org/article/following-tradition-started-by-fidel-cubas-new-president-visits-harlem/.

142. "Castro Stay in Harlem Denounced by Powell," *New York Times*, September 26, 1960.
143. Peter D. Bunzel, "Equal Rights for Negroes Cheered at Tabernacle Rally: Roy Wilkins Says Fight Was Started Late—Must Win Now," *Vineyard Gazette*, July 31, 1962.

Chapter Nine

144. Brooke, Obama, Cowan, Harris, and Booker; Hiram Rhodes Revels was a guest of Governor William Claflin, Oak Bluffs homeowner.
145. Edward W. Brooke, oral history interview with by Linsey Lee of the Martha's Vineyard Museum, August 2007, published as "Finding Island Inspiration and a Place to Gather," *Vineyard Gazette*, January 8, 2015.
146. Mike Seccombe, "Edward Brooke Reflects on Long Political Career," *Vineyard Gazette*, September 7, 2007.
147. Skip Finley, "An Island Apart but with a History of Inclusiveness," *Vineyard Gazette*, February 5, 2018.
148. Skip Finley, "No Barriers to Big Dreams Thanks to Trailblazing Political Rock Star," *Vineyard Gazette*, January 9, 2015.
149. Stan Hart, "Remembering Lucy Bideau, and Her Infectious Spirit," *Vineyard Gazette*, October 8, 2009, https://vineyardgazette.com/news/2009/10/08/remembering-lucy-bideau-and-her-infectious-spirit.
150. Water Robinson, "Giving Thanks to Islanders Who Stood Up against Racism," *Vineyard Gazette*, August 31, 2017, https://vineyardgazette.com/news/2017/08/31/giving-thanks-islanders-who-stood-against-racism.
151. "Bideau Abbot: Honest, Giving and True," *Vineyard Gazette*, October 15, 2009, https://vineyardgazette.com/obituaries/2009/10/16/bideau-abbot-honest-giving-and-true.
152. Hart, "Remembering Lucy Bideau."
153. "Justine Priestley, 83, Was a Pioneering Journalist," *Vineyard Gazette*, August 9, 2004.
154. Zachary Block, "This Is My Country, This Is My Fight, Too: Justine Tyrrell Priestley '43," *Brown Alumni Magazine*, June 21, 2007, https://www.brownalumnimagazine.com/articles/2007-06-21/this-is-my-country-this-is-my-fight-too-justine-tyrrell-priestley-43.
155. Priestly, *By Gertrude Wilson*, frontispiece.
156. Mark Allen Lovewell, "Friends, Old Foes Fete Linda Marinelli," *Vineyard Gazette*, November 19, 2009; "Linda Marinelli Was Longtime Community Leader," *Vineyard Gazette*, January 31, 2013; Julia Wells, "Linda Marinelli Gave Voice to Life," *Vineyard Gazette*, February 7, 2013.

Chapter Ten

157. "Lola's Welcome Mat," *Vineyard Gazette*, September 27, 2018, https://vineyardgazette.com/news/2018/09/27/lolas-welcome-mat.
158. Cheryl Finley in discussion with the author.

Chapter Eleven

159. Douglas Martin, "A'lelia Nelson, 82, President of a Black Cosmetics Company," *New York Times*, February 14, 2001.

BIBLIOGRAPHY

Abrams, Alan, ed. *Black and Free: The Free Negro in America, 1830—A Commentary on Carter Woodson's Negro Heads of Families in the United States in 1830*. Sylvania, OH: Doubting Thomas Publishing, 2001.
Amaral, Pat. *They Plowed the Seas: Profiles of Azorean Master Mariners*. St. Petersburg, FL: Valkyrie Press, 1978.
Banks, Charles Edward. *History of Martha's Vineyard, Dukes County, Massachusetts*. 3 vols. Boston: G.H. Dean, 1911–25.
Bayne, Bijan. *Martha's Vineyard Basketball: How a Resort League Defied Notions of Race and Class*. Lanham, MD: Rowman & Littlefield, 2015.
Bellencampi, Suzan. *Martha's Vineyard: A Field Guide to Island Nature*. Edgartown, MA: Vineyard Stories, 2014.
Brooke, Edward W. *Bridging the Divide: My Life*. New Brunswick, NJ: Rutgers University Press, 2007.
Campisi, Jack. *Martha's Vineyard Camp Meeting Association, 1835–1985*. Oak Bluffs, MA: Martha's Vineyard Camp Meeting Association, 1984.
———. *The Mashpee Indians: Tribe on Trial*. Syracuse, NY: Syracuse University Press, 1991.
Dagnall, Sally W. *Circle of Faith: The Story of the Martha's Vineyard Camp-Meeting*. Edgartown, MA: Vineyard Stories, 2010.
Davis, Charles C. "A Place to Stand to Full Size: The Black Community of Oak Bluffs." BA thesis, Swarthmore College, 2017. http://hdl.handle.net/10066/19167.
Dresser, Thomas. *African Americans on Martha's Vineyard: From Enslavement to Presidential Visit*. Charleston, SC: The History Press, 2010.
———. *Martha's Vineyard: A History*. Charleston, SC: The History Press, 2015.

Bibliography

———. *The Wampanoag Tribe of Martha's Vineyard: Colonization to Recognition.* Charleston, SC: The History Press, 2011.

———. *Whaling on Martha's Vineyard.* Charleston, SC: The History Press, 2018.

Foster, David R. *A Meeting of Land and Sea: Nature and the Future of Martha's Vineyard.* New Haven: Yale University Press, 2017.

Hale, Anne. *Moraine to Marsh: A Field Guide to Martha's Vineyard.* Vineyard Haven, MA: Watership Gardens, 1988.

Hall, Henry, ed. *America's Successful Men of Affairs: The City of New York.* New York: New York Tribune, 1895–96.

Hayden, Robert C., and Karen E. Hayden. *African Americans on Martha's Vineyard and Nantucket: A History of People, Places and Events.* Boston: Select Publications, 1999.

Hine, C.G. *The Story of Martha's Vineyard, from the Lips of Its Inhabitants, Newspaper Files and Those Who Have Visited Its Shores, Including Stray Notes on Local History and Industries.* New York: Hine Brothers, 1908.

Horwitz, Tony. *A Voyage Long and Strange: Rediscovering the New World.* New York: Henry Holt, 2008.

Hough, Henry Beetle. *Martha's Vineyard: Photographs by Alfred Eisenstaedt.* New York: Viking Press, 1975.

———. *Martha's Vineyard: Summer Resort, 1835–1935.* Rutland, VT: Tuttle Pub., 1936.

Huntington, Gale. *An Introduction to Martha's Vineyard and ad Guided Tour of the Island.* Oak Bluffs, MA: Martha's Vineyard Printing Company, 1969.

Jennings, Francis. *The Invasion of America: Indians, Colonialism, and the Cant of Control.* New York: Norton, 1976.

Jones, Peter A. *Oak Bluffs: The Cottage City Years on Martha's Vineyard.* Charleston, SC: Arcadia Publishing, 2007.

Lee, Linsey. *Vineyard Voices: Words, Faces and Voices of Island People.* Edgartown, MA: Martha's Vineyard Historical Society, 1998

Murphy, Jim. *Gone A-Whaling: The Lure of the Sea and the Hunt for the Great Whale.* New York: Clarion Books, 1998.

Nelson, Jill. *Finding Martha's Vineyard: African Americans Home on an Island.* New York: Doubleday, 2005.

Norton, Henry Franklin. *Martha's Vineyard, Historic, Legendary, Scenic.* Hartford: H.F. Norton, R.E. Pyne, 1923.

Parham, Kevin. *The Vineyard We Knew: A Recollection of Summers on Martha's Vineyard.* Plymouth, MA: Pria Publishing, 2014.

Philbrick, Nathaniel. *Mayflower: A Story of Courage, Community, and War.* New York: Viking, 2006.

Pierce, Richard A., and Jerome D. Segal. *The Wampanoag Families of Martha's Vineyard: The Wampanoag Genealogical History of Martha's Vineyard, Massachusetts.* 2 vols. Berwin Heights, MD: Heritage Books, 2003–16.

Powell, Isabel Washington, with Joyce Burnett. *Adam's Belle: A Memoir of Love without Bounds.* Springfield, MA: DBM Press, 2008.

Bibliography

Priestley, Justine. *By Gertrude Wilson: Dispatches of the 1960s from a White Writer in a Black World*. Edgartown, MA: Vineyard Stories, 2005.

Railton, Arthur. *History of Martha's Vineyard: How We Got to Where We Are*. Beverly, MA: Commonwealth Editions, 2006.

Saunders, James R., and Renae N. Shackelford. *The Dorothy West Martha's Vineyard: Stories, Essays, and Reminiscences by Dorothy West Writing in the "Vineyard Gazette."* Jefferson, NC: McFarland, 2001.

Shearer, Stephen Michael. *Gloria Swanson: The Ultimate Star*. New York: Thomas Dunne Books/St. Martin's Press, 2013.

Simmons, William S. *Spirit of the New England Tribes: Indian History and Folklore, 1620–1984*. Hanover, NH: University Press of New England, 1986.

Stacy, Bonnie. *Martha's Vineyard*. Charleston, SC: Arcadia Publishing, 2014.

Starbuck, Alexander. *History of the American Whale Fishery from Its Earliest Inception to the Year 1876*. Waltham, MA: printed by the author, 1878.

Stewart, George R. *Names on the Land: A Historical Account of Place-Naming in the United States*. New York: New York Review Books, 2008.

Stoddard, Chris. *A Centennial History of Cottage City*. Oak Bluffs, MA: Oak Bluffs Historical Commission, 1980.

Taylor, Richard L. *Martha's Vineyard: Race, Property and the Power of Place*. N.p., 2016.

Tolles, Bryant F., Jr. *Summer by the Seaside: The Architecture of New England Coastal Resort Hotels, 1820–1950*. Hanover, NH: University Press of New England, 2008.

Tully, Leslie Hurd. *Martha's Vineyard Island Reflections*. Vol. 1. Oak Bluffs, MA: Hurd Publishing, 2005.

Vineyard Open Land Foundation. *Looking at the Vineyard: A Visual Study for a Changing Island*. West Tisbury, MA: Vineyard Open Land Foundation, 1973.

Walton, Jocelyn Coleman. *The Place My Heart Calls Home: Stories of a Working Class African American Family from Boston to Martha's Vineyard*. Oak Bluffs, MA: A Nickel Down, 2018.

Weintraub, Elaine C., and Carrie C. Tankard. *Lighting the Trail: African American Heritage Trail of Martha's Vineyard*. Oak Bluffs, MA: African American Heritage Trail History Project, 2005.

Weiss, Ellen. *City in the Woods: The Life and Design of an American Camp Meeting on Martha's Vineyard*. Boston: Northeastern University Press, 1998.

West, Dorothy. *Last Leaf of Harlem: Selected and Newly Discovered Fiction by the Author of "The Wedding."* Edited by Lionel C. Bascom. New York: St. Martin's Press, 2008.

———. *The Living Is Easy*. Boston: Houghton, Mifflin, 1948.

———. *The Richer, the Poorer: Stories, Sketches, and Reminiscences*. New York: Doubleday, 1995.

———. *The Wedding*. New York: Doubleday, 1995.

Wonning, Paul R. *A Year of Colonial American Frontier History: A Daily Pioneer History of the American Colonial Frontier*. N.p.: Paul R. Wonning, 2015.

ABOUT THE AUTHOR

 Skip Finley's career in media began in 1971. In addition to serving the leadership of the major broadcast industry associations, the popular executive was responsible for forty-three radio stations (four of which he owned) encompassing seventeen U.S. markets. His work has included business successes with radio networks, syndicated programs, formats and a satellite channel. Finley was a frequent contributor to radio industry trade publications.

Retired, today he is a writer and works for the Vineyard Gazette Media Group as director of sales and marketing and is a guest columnist. He is a member of the Martha's Vineyard Museum Board of Directors.

From June 22, 2012, to June 16, 2017, Finley wrote the *Vineyard Gazette*'s weekly Oak Bluffs Town Column. Thanks to the *Vineyard Gazette*'s circulation of 11,500, his 253 columns were read over 67,000 times, according to Google Analytics, often recording online comments.

In addition to the *Vineyard Gazette*, he is a regular contributor to *Martha's Vineyard Magazine*, *Martha's Vineyard Island Weddings* and the Martha's Vineyard Museum publication *MVMuseum Quarterly* (formerly the *Dukes County Intelligencer*).

There is more information and references at www.skipfinley.com.

www.ingramcontent.com/pod-product-compliance
Lightning Source LLC
Chambersburg PA
CBHW042140160426
43201CB00021B/2347